MW01221877

FOR KURT, WHO HAS MY HEART

First published in 2006 by Simply Read Books
Copyright © Agnes Baumkirchner 2006

Library and Archives Canada Cataloguing in Publication
Baumkirchner, Agnes, 1926-
Whistler Mountain has my soul / Agnes Baumkirchner.
ISBN-10: 0-9688768-6-2
ISBN-13: 978-0-9688768-6-2
1. Baumkirchner, Agnes, 1926- --Homes and haunts--British
Columbia--Whistler Mountain. 2. Whistler Mountain (B.C.). I.Title.
FC3845.W49Z49 2006   971.11'31   C2005-907163-X
10 9 8 7 6 5 4 3 2 1

Cover illustration © A. Matsoureff
Design by Jody de Haas
Printed in Canada

We gratefully acknowledge the support of the Canada Council for the Arts for our publishing program.

WHISTLER
MOUNTAIN
HAS MY SOUL

A MEMOIR BY AGNES BAUMKIRCHNER

CHAPTER ONE

MARCH 1939 – 1938

This morning, the clock on the church steeple of Oberpullendorf – a little Austrian village – showed half past seven. I waited as usual for my friends, watching the familiar scene on the village's single main street. We would all meet there and then walk up the hill, the only hill in town, to the little school in time for the start of lessons at eight o'clock. This morning, the rays of the sun gleamed on the milliner's window, where she was busily arranging the hats. She did this every morning, and I suspected she took the hats home with her each evening and brought them back to the shop each morning. Next door, the butcher was hanging half a pig in his window. Across the street, the shoemaker stood in his doorway, watching the familiar passing scene: the schoolchildren, the towns women wearing their customary kerchiefs tied firmly against the wind I wondered as I saw them: "Who buys the milliner's hats, when all the women seem to wear kerchiefs?"

This morning the scene was subtly different: the bakeshop had not yet opened, and I missed the tantalizing, familiar morning aroma of fresh-baked bread. And why were all these farmers in town, standing around, and not working in the fields?

Ah, but here is Lisa, running towards me, her pigtails flying; she is always late. Coming behind her are Kathrin and Rudy, riding on the milkwagon. The horses seem restless today. Now we are all assembled, waiting only for Judith. We had enough time to spare, so we decided to wait just a little longer for Judith; we all liked her, and didn't want her to feel hurt that we had gone on ahead without her.

We stood waiting, sharing Kathrin's bonbons that she had received for her birthday, watching the townspeople and listening to the old people speaking in Hungarian. Oberpullendorf is close to the Hungarian border, and most of the old people speak only Hungarian; they never liked the idea that the area was ceded to Austria a long time ago. They would have preferred to remain Hungarians.

I checked the time again on the church clock. "Let's go," I suggested.

"Without Judith?" the rest chorused.

"She most likely is ill and not coming or she'd be here by now."

Suddenly, we all heard it – drums, in the distance and coming closer.

"Let's watch; maybe it's a parade!"

"But what parade? It's not May or Christmas," said Kathrin.

Rudi reminded us that if we did not start for school we would be late, but the rest of us decided to wait at least until we could see what the drums heralded.

"There...look...around the corner!" we all cried.

Stretched across the whole street was a huge foreign flag, blood red with a strange twisted cross in the middle. It was the first swastika I had seen, and was carried by two chimney-sweeps, followed by men in brown shirts. The people who lined the street just stood there gaping – they had no idea what it was all about – but they would soon find out!

We were given that day off from school, and many more days that followed. When we finally did return to school nearly everybody's life had changed. The few Jewish pupils we had never returned to school, and I never saw Judith, lively Judith with the curly hair, again. I missed her very much – she was so much fun and had such pretty things to play with. She left without even saying goodbye, and nobody could explain to my satisfaction why, when we were all such good friends, she would do that.

School had changed, too – we didn't have prayers in the morning, and we sang different songs, marching songs. It took some time to get used to the changes, especially to the greeting, which was really strange to us. You stretched out your arm, up above your head, and by the time you had greeted all your teachers and friends this way, you had a sore arm!

One day my parents announced we were moving to another town. Surely they had a reason; I just couldn't understand it. My father was in the hotel and restaurant business, and he bought a restaurant in Wiener Neustadt, far away form the old village. I didn't want to go and leave all my friends and relatives – this was the town of my birth!

"Why do we have to move away?" I thought resentfully. "It must have to do with that new flag." Every time I passed a swastika I had a feeling it was responsible for disrupting my life, and I hated it.

I did not like our new restaurant – it was right next to the railroad station. When I opened my bedroom window, I could almost touch the trains. I used to watch them go by and wonder where everyone was going. Many times I sat daydreaming by my window, and once, when my aunt came to visit, I told her that some day I would go to Canada on those trains, to visit my cousin. My aunt had often spoken of her son, my cousin, who had gone so far away – to Vancouver, British Columbia. Usually when she spoke of him, she did so with tears in her eyes and I would comfort her: "Don't cry, Auntie. I will go to Canada and tell Joe about you and everybody at home."

The townspeople in Wiener Neustadt seemed friendly enough and were very helpful to my parents; but here were so many new people, and the unfamiliar faces were frightening. Where were all my old friends and what were they doing now?

So I sat, blissfully dreaming at my window, while clouds of war gathered around the world. Suddenly – fighting everywhere! And then the bombings started – cities – towns – our town. The first bombing was terrible – no warning – no alarm. Ours was the first Austrian city to be attacked, and we just were not prepared. But people get used to he strangest things, and we got used to those bombings – and survived! Going to the bomb shelters become routine – we just ran to them at the first sound of sirens or aeroplanes.

Sometimes, at night, my father would get confused by the lights. At the slightest danger, the city would be blacked out and the lights at the railway station would be dimmed (we could see this from our windows). But a strong wind could also dim the lights, and since my father took no chances with his family's safety, we would sometimes have to get up on a windy night and run from our warm beds to the cold, empty cellar. "Oh, Dad, I was having such a nice dream!"

The bombings continued, but so also did other aspects of life. I went to school; my father ran his restaurant; trains came and went; babies were born. And in our family, there was bad news: My mother had to go to hospital for a breast cancer operation. So young, just thirty-five! But she seemed quite reconciled to the ordeal, and smiled encouragingly at us as we left her in the hospital room.

We had just returned home when we heard that familiar awesome sound – aeroplanes, coming closer. I ran to the window to watch and listen. There was the siren! And then all hell broke loose. We made it to the cellar just as the first bombs dropped and huddled in the midst of people who prayed, sang or shouted while the building swayed and shook. We all feared it would collapse, but once again it protected us. For our family, our thoughts were all with our mother.

When the raid was over and we ventured out into the sunlight, we saw a horrifying sight – the city was burning! "My God, the hospital!" we cried. But miraculously, it still stood, though most of the doctors and nurses had evacuated it. But one doctor and one nurse stayed on and in the midst of the raid had performed a successful operation on my mother. Incredible! If there are miracles in this world, I believe that was one of them.

After a few days in hospital, my mother came home, and we hired a car to drive out of the city. If there were an air raid, she would not be able to run fast enough to reach the bomb shelter. "Run for your life!" had become our motto, with a grim reality.

"We are given but one life, and mine hasn't even begun! Oh God," I prayed, "give us peace!"

But my fervent prayer was not answered that night, nor for many many more, and the sirens wailed again. We drove away from the city, as the bombers droned overhead – the sky was filled with them – and the ground flack attacked them. It was a spectacular sight for those with the stamina to watch. It lasted several hours and then, suddenly, it was quiet.

When the raid ended, we were anxious to return to our home in the city from our country hiding-place (safer now than the bomb shelters). My mother was having pains from her recent operation and my feet ached. But as we neared our house we stared as if in a dream – or nightmare. It was in ruins. "It can't be!" I wailed. "All our things – my clothes, my books – the cats and our dog!" I looked to my parents for answers and guidance, but saw that they were just as lost as I. Mother held my hand, but I snatched it away and ran toward the ruins, looking for something – anything. It was far too dangerous, and Mama pulled me away.

We spent that night in a hotel, one of the few still standing, and the next day my father decided we would go West. We gathered together our few remaining possessions and started marching along with thousands of other people: Poles, Hungarians, Romanians, and livestock: horses, cows, pigs. It was one long, endless line of homeless humanity. Nobody really knew where we were going. We just kept marching, sleeping in barns, on streets, in forests, wherever we were in whatever was available. The war raged on around us, but we were beyond caring.

I asked my father once were we were going, and he said, "To the mountains." What mountains? It was flat country here, only a few hills. I didn't understand, as I had never seen mountains before. I wasn't sure if I liked the idea. But like it or not, there was nowhere else to go.

Often we had to run for cover. The aeroplanes were overhead again, but not bombers this time. These planes would fly low, strafing the line of refugees; sometimes we could even see the pilots. These planes were Russians, and they loved playing hide-and –seek with us, appearing suddenly beside the road. The American planes at least gave us some warning of their coming, so we could hide. I was always relieved when night came. Sometimes we found a barn, warm and friendly with the smell of the cows and hay.

I don't know how long we were on the road – weeks – months – it seemed like years. Then suddenly the landscape changed, and the air grew cooler. At last, in the distance, we saw them – the majestic mountains! They commanded, if not immediate love, at least immediate respect. They appeared higher and higher as we came closer and closer. We reached the town of Bishofshofen, and I remember it well, for it was the first time we slept in a bed again in a hotel. But our comfort was short-lived; there was an air raid that night (which was to be the last one on that city) and once again we were on the move.

After some sleep, we headed toward Badgastein, a very expensive resort town. We hadn't much money – just some jewellery – but we got a nice room in a pension. Our landlady was very kind and understanding, and gave us all the help she could. There were other people staying there, in the same circumstances as we, and we became a big family.

Now when I looked out my window, there were no trains or railroads – just mountains. How strange and wonderful were those friendly giants!

We had no more air raids in the shelter of the mountains, although the war was not yet over. We heard that the Americans were not far away. The Russians had advanced to Weiner Neustadt, our hometown, and the British and the French were also advancing.

In spite of the news of the war and advancing armies, we lived a nearly normal life. Badgastein became our home, and we enjoyed its difference from our life on the Austrian plains.

Badgastein, in the Land of Salzburg, was a resort and spa. People came here for skiing in the winter, and the sick came to "take the waters," which supposedly had medicinal properties. It was an expensive resort, as I mentioned, and really not the place for poor refugees, but people understood our difficulties and didn't seem to mind if bills went unpaid.

I had grown to like Badgastein, and become used to the mountains; in fact my brother and I climbed them and even reached the height where the edelweiss grew. We discovered all sorts of things. The flowers were quite different in colour and shape from those back home and in the spring, the meadows were blanketed by yellow buttercups.

It was such a day in May 1945, when I went to the grocery store to do some errands for Mama. Suddenly the church bells started ringing, and people on the streets were hugging and kissing each other in celebration, laughing and crying at the same time. "Will somebody please tell me what's going on?' I asked a passerby.

"But haven't you heard?" he shouted. "THE WAR IS OVER!"

And not long after that, those friendly American soldiers marched into the village.

My father was pleased by this turn of events, for he was sure to get a job since he spoke fluent English.

We had lost everything, had been without work for so long, and the summer was fast passing and winter approached. I had no coat. But the Americans came to our aid with great generosity. How excited I was the day the tall, handsome American officer with a black moustache took me to army headquarters to select needed clothing. Oh, the mountains of clothing! Coats! Shoes! Hats! Everything was there. Suddenly I was a girl again, playing dress-up, eagerly trying on this and that. It was such fun! I just couldn't decide which coat to take, but finally chose a black one that looked like a Persian lamb. As it was cold that day, I decided to wear it home. In fact, it had started to snow as I left the barracks, and I thought let it snow! I was warm in my nice coat!

The lighted store windows, all dressed to tempt the Christmas shoppers, beckoned and I stopped once more to look at the nice things. "Oh, if only I had some money, and could buy those lovely gifts for my family!"

As I stood there, I put my cold hands into my coat pockets. Something in one pocket tore and I felt my spirits drop – my coat seemed to be falling apart already.

"But wait, that's not the lining – there's something else!" I reached deeper and felt some paper. I pulled out an envelope, and under the street lamp, I opened it, and couldn't believe my eyes. There was a Christmas card saying, Merry Christmas – Edna House, 121 Graystone Drive, Hagerstown, MD and folded inside was a ten-dollar bill!

My father worked in Badgastein for a short time, but when the opportunity arose to manage a castle in Salzburg, he couldn't resist it and so in summer of 1948 we moved to Salzburg. And in Salzburg, I fell in love!

Chapter Two
Kurt

His name was Kurt. He spoke differently, a different dialect. In Salzburg, people dressed differently, too – each province had its own identity.

Kurt was a very charming man. He had curly blond hair, cut short, and he looked a little pale – due no doubt to his recent interment in a Russian prison camp. He had a very high forehead, and it was difficult to determine the colour of his eyes – in some light they looked gray, and then again in some light I thought they had a hint of green. Kurt showed me all the beautiful sights and sounds in and around Salzburg, and one day as we sat in a favourite café, he told me how he was captured.

It actually happened after the war ended.

"The war was over – the rumour had spread among the troops. The war was over – but not for us! We were ordered to hold our position and not surrender. I was in the German army, although an Austrian citizen, and had been in the thick of the fighting for some time. But this, now, this did not make sense! I longed to return to Salzburg to see my family. The army was falling apart and everybody was on his own; soldiers moved in all directions, drifting sometimes directly into the arms of the enemy. My location was somewhere in Czechoslovakia and the Russians were closing in on us.

It was a beautiful day, and I had just taken off my jacket when I heard shouted orders in a foreign language. I listened again, and the shouts came from all sides, like an echo. The next thing I knew, I was a prisoner of war, even though the war was over!

We were marched off to a camp behind the Russian lines. I tried to figure our exact location, to make plans to escape. I felt we were not far from the Austrian border. A fellow-countryman decided to risk it with me, so one very wet night we made a bid for freedom. The camp was unfenced and poorly guarded, so it was not too difficult."

At this point in Kurt's narrative the waiter interrupted to ask if we would like more *Kuchen*. I had already eaten two pieces, but even though it was getting late I ordered a third and asked Kurt to continue his story, for I had become too absorbed in it to let him stop now!

"Well, we had marched for some time when we came upon a group of women, who began crying and screaming and came running toward us, asking if they could join us. They were fleeing the Russian soldiers too. I tried to reassure them, but they had been listening to too many wild tales. That was all we needed – a bunch of hysterical women!

We decided to sleep in the trees for safety. I made myself as comfortable as I could, and as I looked through the trees I thought I could see Austria. I dozed off, and was awakened by barking dogs. It was too late to escape. I was recaptured, taken to Russia where I spent three years in a prisoner of war camp. I came back just a little while ago."

I studied Kurt's face for signs of excitement, anxiety or remembered fear, but his expression was impassive. I came to the conclusion that he was not too emotional. Yet, though he had told his story in a monotone voice, he exuded confidence and self-assurance, and I liked that.

The seasons passed. Kurt and I had been seeing each other for two years when Kurt asked me to marry him. It was just before Christmas, and I thought that would be a nice time to get engaged.

"You know that I would say yes," I said to him, "but I have to ask my parents. We will ask them when you come over on my birthday. They asked me to invite you."

"When is your birthday?"

"Have you forgotten already? It's December 13."

"Oh, *ja*," he joked. "You have birthday and Christmas almost at the same time!"

Kurt arrived on my birthday carrying a large parcel, one he just couldn't hide. It contained a pair of skis. I was rather puzzled by this choice of gift as I didn't ski and had really expected an engagement ring! My mother said, "You'll break your leg with those things!"

Though Kurt's gift received an unenthusiastic reception, he nevertheless insisted that I keep the skis and promised to teach me to ski.

My parents had been quite happy at the news of our engagement, though as puzzled as I that I should be given skis instead of a ring.

"I guess he can't afford both," I reasoned, "and skiing is healthy."

During the Christmas holidays, we went to Badgastein. I loved the idea of returning to those friendly mountains...but not to ski! However, Kurt gave me no choice.

It was very cold and icy on the beginners' "bunny hill". After a couple of attempts I gave up the sport for good that first day. But on the second day, we were at it again! I think Kurt never realized how clumsy I was. I could not stand on those darned skis even one minute. Kurt would be standing talking to me, and the next minute he would be standing talking to himself as I slid down the hill screaming. It was embarrassing. Then, to further complicate the situation, I would take off my skis and climb up toward him, all the while being shouted at by other skiers that I was ruining the runs with my boots. Once back atop the slope, Kurt started yelling at me too, and had we been married at that time I would have asked for a divorce. How could anybody take skiing that seriously?

In the evenings we would sit at the bar; actually, I would sort of hang over the barstool, my body a mass of aches and pains and bruises, and I wondered if Kurt and I really had anything in common. But he was very charming and gallant and in the end, won me all over again.

"Don't worry," he would say, "You'll get the hang of it. Skiing is a lot of fun!"

"How long have you been skiing?" I asked.

"Oh, all my life I guess."

We got along fine in the bar, and in fact off the slopes I really liked being with him. As if guessing my thoughts were warming toward him, he asked, "What do you think? When should we get married?"

I liked that subject much better.

"Well, next year," I said. "This one is almost over."

We stayed a few more days in Badgastein and I was relieved, in a sense, when the ski lessons ended and we had to leave.

•••

We were married on February 8, 1951 in a small chapel in a castle which was a popular place for weddings. Family and friends were there, but it was not a large wedding. I wore a green suit instead of a white wedding gown. It would have been too expensive to have one made, and we could not buy one. Actually, we all wore coats as it was very cold. Mama made a nice buffet for the reception and I did get a ring, too. Next day, we both went to work as usual.

Chapter Three
To Canada

One fine spring day, as I walked hand-in-hand with my new husband through the park, Kurt abruptly stopped at a bench and suggested we sit. I was glad I was sitting when he posed his amazing question: "Would you like to move to Canada with me?"

I would have been surprised had he suggested Italy or Switzerland, but Canada! In North America! All I knew about Canada was that my cousin Joe had gone there many years ago, and though he corresponded regularly with his family, he couldn't come back, nor could they visit him. It was too far away, and the journey was too expensive. Even so, it would be exciting to visit America!

"I can't give you an answer right away – I don't know – I have to ask my parents – Oh God, my parents! I can't ask them – that's crazy – it's too far – much too far!"

"It would be sort of a honeymoon trip," he joked.

"Sure – a honeymoon of no return."

"No, no, we would come back if things got better in Austria again; we'd stay just a for a little while."

Our parents were shocked at the news of our decision to emigrate. I told them that at this point, we didn't even know if we would be accepted, and it would take some time to get our traveling papers together. By the time all was in readiness, I hoped everyone would have become used to the idea.

We put in our application and I obtained some books about Canada – but even researching those books, I couldn't comprehend how vast a country I would be entering.

Salzburg was full of immigrants waiting to go to the United States and Canada. At the time I was working at the American Central Intelligence Office, where people were screened for political and/or criminal backgrounds before being issued visas. I witnessed the heartbreak of families being split up – some members allowed to emigrate right away, others to follow later, and some never to be allowed to leave. Did I really want to emigrate? I didn't think I could go through with it. In my confusion, I avoided my parents and brothers. Maybe, I feared and half-hoped, we wouldn't get a visa, and the decision would be made for us.

America was the land of unlimited opportunities. But we had been at war with these people – how would they accept us now? It was only a few years since the war had ended – had the wounds healed? I wasn't sure.

No matter how I rationalized and agonized, Kurt was adamant. He had made up his mind. So I finally agreed, because with Kurt beside me, I was sure everything would work out fine.

While we waited for our visas, we started packing, which wasn't easy as we weren't allowed to take much with us – nor could we take much money. I had a big trunk standing open in my room, reminding all who passed it of our insane idea. But it was no longer just an idea – preparations were well underway, and it seemed nothing could stop us now.

My mother worried that I would be cold, and I tried to reassure her by saying that it would be for a little while only, then we would be back in Austria. My father collected money for us – in all shapes and sizes – not too many dollars, but all kinds of other currencies, even though I reminded him that in Canada they accepted dollars only.

One day, as I was busily stuffing a big eiderdown quilt into the trunk, Kurt rushed in to tell me that he had obtained our visas. Not only the visas, but a job as well! It seems they were looking for engineers in Canada, but since he didn't speak English, they suggested he start out as a drafts-man. And we were not going to Vancouver, but to Toronto. I was disappointed at that, as I had been hoping to go to Vancouver, where my cousin Joe lived.

In September 1951, we were finally ready to leave. My heart pounded with anticipation and ached for all I was leaving behind. Now I com-forted, not my mother but myself by repeating that it would be for a little while only – that I would be back home again soon. I cried myself to sleep that last night and had terrible dreams. Then came the morning – our last breakfast as a family, and nobody could eat a thing. I was glad when Kurt arrived and we all left for the railway station.

All our friends and relatives were at the station to see us off. The only one missing was Kurt's younger brother, who was coming on his bicycle.

There was my father with his snow-white hair. "Will I see him again? He looks so old today." He handed us a handkerchief full of money. "Here you are, darling," he said to me. "If you don't like it you can always come home." Kurt jokingly replied that he hoped there was enough money for his return fare too!

My mother kept telling us to dress warmly – you'd think we were going to the North Pole!

My aunt handed us a bundle of letters and photographs to give to cousin Joe.

Then we heard the whistle of the train – it was coming! I thought my heart would stop! The huffing and puffing of the engine suddenly reminded me of all those times I used to sit by my window in Weiner Neustadt and watch trains go by. And one will take me to Canada – at least as far as the ship.

Kurt was saying his farewells with hugs and kisses. Then it was my turn. We were all crying, except for Kurt; I had never seen him cry – he was so strong! His brother had not yet arrived, but the conductor was shouting *"Einsteigen!"* and closing the doors of the carriages. We had to board the train, we couldn't wait for him. Mama wouldn't let go of my hand until I told her I would open the window as soon as I got on the train. Then my younger brother held my hand, pressing something into it – something soft and wet and tiny – an edelweiss, like those we climbed the sheltering mountains to pick so many years ago! My cheeks were wet as I treasured this little flower of my Austria.

Once aboard the train, I put my hand out the open train window, and my mother grasped it again, and even after the train started moving she ran along beside us as long as she could, still holding my hand. And everyone shouted, *"Auf Wiedersetien! Auf Wiedersetien!"* And we were on our way.

CHAPTER FOUR

BOUND FOR TORONTO

We stayed by the window, Kurt holding my hand, looking toward the mountains which he had so often climbed and skied. Suddenly we saw someone silhouetted against the mountain backdrop – someone with a bicycle, waving a cap. It was Kurt's brother, giving us our final send-off. Kurt was squeezing my had so hard I thought it would break – but I understood. What a beautiful country – we must be out of our minds to leave it!

As the train progressed toward the coast, people boarded and left at each stop. We were the only ones going all the way to Bremerhaven, where our ship, the *Anna Salen*, was waiting.

The scenery was changing now, and so were the people. We noticed more fishermen. They were friendly, but we had trouble understanding them. They spoke German, but in a different dialect – I hadn't known that the German language could change every few miles.

At last came our call to leave the train. What a relief! My body ached from the long hours of sitting. We went to the *Ueberseeheim*, which is a place where we could leave our luggage, wait for the ship, and sleep if necessary.

Now I fully realized just how many people were going to Canada – all nationalities – whole families, from small children to the very old. We deposited our luggage at the *Ueberseeheim* and went sightseeing. Never having been far from home, everything was interesting to me, and since we had so much German and European currency, we decided to spend it. It would be worthless in Canada.

We ate in the finest restaurants, went to the movies, and one evening went to a circus. That night we decided to stay in a hotel – after all, we were on our honeymoon! And what a hotel we chose – when they showed us our room I thought this must be what heaven looked like! Pink eiderdown quilts on a huge bed with carved ivory headboards and sheets draped like clouds on the ceiling. Soft music drifted from somewhere, and there was champagne on the table. I'm sure we got the bridal suite.

As the sun shone into our room the next morning there was a knock on the door and a maid entered with breakfast. "I think there must be some mistake, " I said to Kurt. "Maybe they think we're the Rothschilds." But Kurt assured me there was no mistake – he had ordered the breakfast, as he remembered my saying once that having breakfast in bed was to me the height of luxury. As we ate, we listened to the news and heard that there had been a big storm in the Atlantic, but it wouldn't affect our departure. We would leave as scheduled.

Later that day we went down to the harbour to have a look at our ship. A luxury liner it was not. This converted freighter had been brought into service along with so many others, to ferry all the displaced persons to their new homes overseas. Before this vessel had been revamped to haul a human cargo, it had probably carried tobacco or fish.

"It must have been fish," I decided, as the sailors showed us to our cabins. Or was that smell coming from the kitchen? My cabin was right next to it.

Being aboard a ship was another first for me, though I had not expected our arrangements to be so primitive. The women were separated from the men, married or not, and assigned a huge cabin furnished with about fifty bunk beds. There were no closets. The toilets were outside along the corridor somewhere. And the dining rooms were furnished more like a diner than like the elegant dining rooms on the luxury liners I had heard about.

But the crew, representing nationalities from every part of Europe, were brisk and friendly, and didn't seem to mind that they were serving on a vessel that was so rusty and old.

The other passengers were all very nice, and some had a good sense of humour. We soon made new friends aboard ship, which was just as well as were going to be living at close quarters for some time.

It was not long before we all were exchanging stories of past lives and future dreams. We all looked forward to mealtime for excitement; and sometimes we had emergency drills. They showed us the lifeboats. Ah, those lifeboats! They really came alive during the evening, as married couples disappeared while walking around the deck.

Seasickness!

My cabin was next to the kitchen and the smell of food was just too much for some of us. Funny thing about seasickness – you're not really that sick, but there isn't anything you can do about it either except wait to get on land again! And there was no land in sight – just water everywhere you looked – water and more water. One day we hit a storm, or a storm hit us, and what a storm it was! The boat was rocking up and down like a toy ship.

• • •

To relieve the tedium, the crew asked for volunteers to help in the kitchen and with the serving of the food. I was in charge of the vegetables and Kurt was serving tea. Poor Kurt – he was forever perspiring from the steaming tea!

One evening someone organized a big party, but hearing all the old familiar songs like *Lili Marlene* and others, so many people got homesick that what should have been a fun evening turned into a sentimental bash!

At night, we did a lot of talking in our cabin. My neighbour, Maria, told me about the single girls on the ship who wakened her when they stole from the cabin during the night seeking illicit adventures – she berated them in the most shocking language! Maria also told me about her finance, Willie – they were going to be married in Canada.

After two and half weeks of seeing nothing but the water of the Atlantic Ocean, it was wonderful to sight land in the distance. It seemed a very tiny land at first, but grew bigger as we neared it. It reminded me of that earlier time when I first saw the mountains.

Though I had studied my map, I did not recognize the land. Some said it was Halifax – some said Montreal. They were all guessing, but it was Halifax and we were passing it en route to Québec City, Québec, where we finally disembarked in October 1951.

Before we said goodbye to our fellow passengers, we were given a very pleasant surprise – each of the volunteers who had helped out on the ship was given twenty-five dollars. It was totally unexpected, and since none of us had much money, this unexpected windfall was most welcome.

We tried to find Marie and Willie and some of the other people we had gotten to know well during the voyage, but the place was bedlam – people seemed to be milling round in circles. We were segregated according to our various destinations, and then there was more waiting for trains, planes or buses.

Our group decided to wander around Quebéc City a bit and have our first look at Canada and its people. It was evening and the streets were ablaze with neon lights. We heard music coming from somewhere that looked like a bar, and as there are always some adventurers in every group, one of us just pushed the door open and in we all went. It was like the *Moulin Rouge* in Paris. We ordered drinks, but the waiters didn't understand our English – and I had studied so hard! But of course, these were French-speaking Canadians, and the majority in Quebéc spoke only French. As no one in our group could speak French, we hurriedly downed the proffered drinks and left.

It was hard to believe – I was actually in Canada, at last! We finally did see Maria and Willie. They were going to Vancouver while we destined for Toronto. I didn't have a cousin in Toronto, but I did have Kurt!

When we boarded the train for Toronto, we recognized a few people from the boat, especially the policeman from Graz. There he sat, still nursing the special little plant his aunt in Canada had requested. She would never know the difficulties of carrying it all the way from Austria: hiding it, watering it and now finally holding it in his hand so no harm would come to it.

We were all sitting up on the benches, very tired, when the conductor came through to tell us that the benches converted into beds. What a happy relief! But we didn't sleep much; we were too busy looking out of the windows, seeing Canada and its people. "They look just like us," said Kurt. I don't know what we had expected – but I hadn't seen one Native person yet and wondered where they were.

Finally I did fall asleep and had the most unusual dream. I dreamed that Kurt and I were walking down the street. He was wearing leather shorts and I had on a dirndl skirt and blouse. People were pointing at us and laughing, and I was so ashamed. Then suddenly there appeared a figure in a long flowing dress with a cape all patterned in maple leaves. She proceeded to drape her cape around us, saying: "Welcome to Canada! I am Mother Canada. Of course, I can only be your stepmother – your real mother is Austria." I woke up with a jolt as the train stopped and the conductor shouted, "Toronto!"

Chapter Five

Settling In

Did I hear correctly? Are we really in Toronto?

I had read a lot about it and remembered it was the largest English-speaking city in Canada. Metropolitan Toronto, which included twelve municipalities, had a population of close to two million at that time, if my book was correct. Looking at the hordes of people in the terminal station, I believed it must be true, and thought how appropriate was the city's Native name, which means "Meeting Place."

Kurt was gathering our things together, and while we were puzzling over what to do next, we saw a group of people coming toward us. It was a welcoming committee – representatives from the Government, interpreters and some local businessmen. For those who did not have a sponsor, job contract or relative, these people would hire immediately. They paid a little less, we found out later, but at the time no one questioned them. We were not worried, because Kurt had a job waiting for him.

A very friendly woman who represented the Government directed us to where food was being offered and accommodation arranged. There was hot chocolate, tea, coffee and a veritable mountain of doughnuts, which soon shrunk into a small hill as the hungry wayfarers descended on it. Then we were driven to a place called Ajax, just outside of Toronto. The housing must have been constructed as an army-camp originally, and it looked a bit neglected. However, we had our own private room; it was warm and spacious, and most importantly, it was free. So was breakfast, lunch and supper. We could stay until we found a job, or for a maximum of fourteen days.

Ajax was a small town and there was not much to see, but to us everything was interesting. For instance, it was fun watching the people at the supermarkets. "Shall we go in?" I asked Kurt, and he agreed. We had a few dollars and decided to spend some of it. First we watched the others for a while and then started loading our own carts. What a difference from the line-ups in our war-torn land just for a loaf of bread, often to find, when it came our turn to be served, that everything was all gone! Here were so many varieties of breads, sausage, cheeses – I felt like a child let loose in a candy shop!

As we walked back to our lodgings, I noticed that there were very few people walking; they all had cars! I had never seen so many cars in my entire life!

After a few days we took a bus to Toronto to see about Kurt's job. Toronto, the Meeting Place! It surely looked that way – there were Italians, Hungarians, Chinese, Japanese and many other nationalities. So different from back home! However, this was no time to get homesick or sentimental; besides, I liked Toronto with its high buildings. But Kurt did not care for the city. There was something missing -- the mountains! It's true, as the saying goes, "You can take the boy from the mountains, but you can't take the mountains from the boy."

We walked up and down Spadina Avenue and up and down Bloor Street, but couldn't find the address we had been given. We decided to have something to eat; but that was not so easy. With our limited English, we couldn't understand the menu, so we finally just pointed at something and were served a very good Spanish Omelet. It surprised us that they didn't serve alcoholic drinks in the restaurant: we had to go somewhere else for wine and beer. As our search for our elusive employer continued, we ate several meals, still without finding a place to have some beer. Kurt was impatient, thirsty and tired, and I had to find a washroom. "Ah, there! It says 'Ladies' on one door and 'Escorts' (whatever that means) on the other." I got some puzzled looks from the other customers when, after walking down the stairs I turned and ran right back up again, yelling to Kurt, "They're drinking beer down there!"

After practically gulping down two bottles of beer, Kurt felt infinitely better. We circled the streets some more and finally, there it was! The address we'd been looking for! But we couldn't believe what they told us – they had been looking for engineers and draftsmen three years ago, but they didn't need anyone right now.

"But, sir," I said, "we've come all the way from Austria, don't you understand, Austria, Europa. We have a contract – please look again." He couldn't believe it either, but there was nothing he could do to help us. We just had to help ourselves! Whatever or whoever was to blame for our predicament, it didn't help us now. We went home very disappointed, and considerably shaken.

Since nobody else could help us, we got a few newspapers and started looking through the help wanted columns every day. We also went to the Employment Office every second day. Our time was running out – we could stay in our present lodging for only fourteen days. Some of the immigrants told us that when they came to Canada they had no place to stay, so we should consider ourselves lucky in that respect. They managed, and so would we in this land of milk and honey – or is it milk and money? We would find out!

It was on one of our trips to the Employment Office that we got lucky. We were in the waiting rooms, as usual, when our names were called. At first I thought they had something for Kurt, but they asked if we would take a domestic job. Domestic? Well, looking after a house and its people; in other words, cook, housekeeper, gardener, etc. We had no choice.

We took the address and asked about directions. One gentleman told us it was just around the corner from the Synagogue. "Synagogue?"

"Yes, this is the Jewish district."

As we walked, I explained it to Kurt who had trouble understanding English.

"They are Jewish."

"Who is Jewish?"

"The people we are going to work for." I remembered my childhood friend, Judith. She was Jewish. Maybe she lived around this district somewhere too. But how would they accept us; the war was not that far behind us. I was sure they hadn't forgotten.

"Maybe we should get something else," I said.

To find our new employers we walked through a district of beautiful homes and gardens. It was like paradise after the ruins we had left behind us. We had never seen manicured lawns like these before. We didn't cut the grass this way at home.

The houses got bigger and bigger. Suddenly I was so homesick I started to cry. Kurt tried to comfort me, but I knew that if I had the money I would have turned right around and gone back home. I tried to stop crying and dried my eyes. Then I saw the street sign: Burnside Drive. That was the street. Now look for the number – I got so nervous I dropped the paper – picked it up and looked at it again – it must be on the other side of the street – there it was – the address matched the one on the paper.

My heart was pounding as I rang the doorbell. A well-built middle-aged man answered the door and I handed him the papers. He asked us in and said he would call his wife. It was noon, but his wife was still in bed. I guessed that must be usual for the rich; and rich they must be. Everything was so beautiful, and so many rooms! "They will not seem so beautiful if you have to clean them all," Kurt whispered.

Suddenly the lady of the house appeared. She came down the stairs in the most magnificent robe I had seen. She was no longer young, but still lovely and slim and smiling. As she showed us through the house, I counted twenty rooms. They all looked so clean, except the kitchen, which was a mess – wall-to-wall dirty dishes! She explained that the last girl got married, and the one before her went back home, but they had all loved it here. When she asked me if I could cook, I said yes, though I was stretching the truth a little. However, with a cookbook, I was sure I could manage. I had to!

Our quarters were downstairs, next to the laundry room. After washing quickly, I donned my uniform and started to work on all those dishes.

In the evening we met the rest of the family – a son and a daughter in their late teens. The girl was overweight and had to have a special diet; most of her food had to be cooked in milk. They ate a lot of kosher food, but were not too strict about it. I remembered eating at Judith's many times, and it was not so very different. However, of necessity, I learned to cook very quickly and in a few days had established a routine which started at 6 am and never finished before midnight. There were twenty rooms plus the bathrooms to clean, plus the cooking, washing and ironing to do. And it seemed they always had guests!

Since Kurt had no job, he helped me. Once, while the family was away for the weekend, he helped with the laundry, while I cleaned the upstairs. They did have a washing machine and dryer, but Kurt had never seen those monsters before. When I went down to see how he was getting along, I found him sorting an unholy mess. He had put red woolen socks in with the white sheets, and of course, the result was a disaster. The white sheets were rainbow-coloured and the rest of the laundry seemed to be completely ruined.

"Not to worry," said Kurt. "I'll fix it." And he did. He poured two or three bottles of bleach into a bathtub full of water, then swished the laundry around in it. The next morning the sheets were white again, but the nylon underwear had disintegrated. We hoped they wouldn't miss it. As a matter of fact, the only comment was that the laundry was lovely, but next time I should use less bleach!

Chapter Six

Guess Who's Coming to Dinner?

We had been with the Jewish family for some time when I began to suffer from stomach trouble. Nothing seemed to taste right, and we blamed the kosher meats. Still, even when Kurt brought me ham from the nearby delicatessen, I couldn't eat it. Finally, I had to see a doctor.

"No, it's not the kosher food, my dear. You're pregnant."

"Pregnant!"

"Now?" blurted Kurt.

"Yes, now. Not later."

"Well, that's just the way it is. We'll just have to look for a job for both of us – something easier for you – maybe in an office. Sooner or later, we'll find it."

It was nearly Christmas – our first Christmas away from home. I was very homesick, especially when the snow came; it reminded me of those snow-capped mountains back home.

One day, as we walked through a department store we saw some people carrying skis. We asked them where they were going to ski, and they replied that they were heading for the Laurentians, in Quebéc. Too far away for us. I knew Kurt was missing the mountains and skiing even more than I was.

The winter was very cold that year. Sometimes the snow was so bad that no cars or buses could move. I had only one coat, a leather one, and used to dry it near the oven every day. One day it was a little too close to the heat and the leather cracked: good-bye leather coat.

In our search for wok, we met some of our countrymen, and they told us that Massey-Harris, manufacturers of tractors and farm equipment were hiring people. Since we hadn't told our employers we were looking for other work, we planned to go on my days off, because Kurt's English was still not too fluent.

The time passed too slowly for Kurt, so he decided to go on his own. When he came home, he asked me what a grinder was.

"A grinder? I don't really know. Let's look it up in the dictionary." But we couldn't find it in the dictionary, so I asked Kurt why he wanted to know about a grinder. Then he told me that while he was sitting in the Massey-Harris waiting room, they called out many different occupations, and each time many hands were raised. Then when they called out "Grinders," no one signaled, so he raised his hand.

"You're crazy, Kurt! There's a penalty for taking a job you know nothing about!"

"Well, we'll worry about that later. I got the job. Now you find something, and we can move out of here and rent a room somewhere."

Our luck held, and I found a job in the Superintendent's office at he University of Toronto. Soon after we also found a room to rent.

As a grinder, Kurt was grinding away pieces on an assembly line, and found it easy work. They even told him to slow down, as he was surpassing the norm.

We had much more leisure together now, and also time to go sightseeing, except when Kurt was on the night shift.

Toronto was a lovely city, and we discovered all its little restaurants – Austrian, Hungarian, Little Denmark – we were beginning to feel at home. But there were no mountains, and Kurt missed them even more than he missed his mother. Once when we were skiing in Austria, he said something I never forgot: "You can have my heart," he said, "but the mountains have my soul."

Finally the long winter was over and the spring came to Canada – the snow was melting, the sun was stronger, the days longer and my stomach bigger. And bigger. It looked as if I were going to have twins. I longed to have my mother with me. We hadn't told them of our expected event back home, as they would be so worried.

We decided to look for a little bigger apartment; with the baby coming, one room might be a little crowded. But what difficulties! There were plenty of rooms advertised in the newspapers, but we were turned down at each one, and didn't understand why. We thought perhaps they didn't like Austrians or Germans. The next time we were turned down we questioned them and couldn't believe what we heard – they didn't want to rent to families with children. And mine wasn't even born yet! But I must confess I looked highly imminent.

I bought a bigger, wider coat, but it didn't help. Finally, after many weeks of hunting, we got a room with an Italian couple – they had eleven children of their own, so one more wouldn't matter. They were very nice people, and most helpful.

It was time for me to get organized for the birth of my child. We had no crib, nor clothes for the baby, nor much money, and I would have to quit working soon. I was accepted at Women's College Hospital, so the birth and hospital stay would be free. I was quite concerned about the other baby needs, though, until a couple from Austria, who lived on our street and had three children of their own, came to our aid. We became very good friends with Mary and Stefan, and asked them to be godparents as they were also Catholic, and they accepted.

But what a lot of things we still needed! My landlady suggested that I open a charge account. I didn't know what a charge account was, but my landlady explained that you bought on time and paid so much a month on your purchases; so, I went to a large department store and applied. I tried to answer all the questions on the application form truthfully – length of residence in Canada, nationality, how much money did my husband earn – on and on. And the result was that I was turned down flat!

Undaunted, I filled in another application form, and this time lied a little: I gave Kurt a raise, said we'd been in Canada a little longer, and that we had a car. And of course, I gave myself an English name. I was Mrs. Brown. And the result? The result was diapers and a crib for our new baby, and a nice robe for me for the hospital.

"Just watch your payments," my friend Mary said. "As long as you pay you'll be okay."

All I could think of was that my baby would have a bed and blankets – I could go to jail later.

It was June 27, 1952 – the hottest day yet in Toronto – when Mary and Stefan rushed me to the hospital. Kurt was working, and even had he been home, he didn't have a car. Mary assured me that there was nothing to worry about – she had three children – but I was still scared, and, after she left, very lonely. I kept calling for my mother, until someone in desperation told me to shut up.

I spent almost the full day in labour, and it was close to midnight when they told me I had a little girl, and she looked like me! How could they tell? She must have red hair. There she was, our little Canadian, our daughter, Vivian.

Kurt came to see me every day and always brought me fruit – didn't he realize I would like some flowers? But Kurt, always the realist, said you can't eat flowers, and there wasn't enough money for both.

Vivian was a beautiful baby, and I would have been quite happy to stay home and care for her. But that was impossible – we needed my salary. I found a lady who had been a nurse and looked after several other children in her home; I felt that she would be the right person to look after Vivian while I was at work.

I found work at a department store as a bookkeeper.

But Kurt was never completely happy in his job – he wanted something in his own field, engineering. I really believe, though, that it was the mountains of British Columbia beckoning that prompted him to sign that contract with Alcan. He came to the office one day and told me that he was going to Kitimat, B.C. As soon as he was settled he would send for me and the baby.

"Besides," he said to mollify me, "That's where your cousin Joe lives."

This was true; cousin Joe lived in Vancouver, and perhaps I could write to him and ask if I could stay there until I could go to Kitimat, or until Kurt was transferred to Vancouver. I read that British Columbia is like Austria, only much bigger, and bordered the ocean. But it was not the ocean that attracted Kurt – nor was it the job at Alcan. He just couldn't live without being surrounded by mountains.

I didn't have long to wait. In the fall of 1952 Kurt sent me an airline ticket, one way from Toronto to Vancouver. He had arranged with my cousin for me to stay there until Kurt moved down from Kitimat and we found a place of our own. With Vivian in my arms I took my first aeroplane trip. The weather was fine, and what little I allowed myself to see of the view was good. I was afraid of looking out the window – we were so high! – and the pockets of turbulence and dishes rattling as a result made me quite uncomfortable. Not being used to this sort of thing, I worried that this big bird might not make it all the way to Vancouver. But the longer I was in the air, the more confident I became.

It seemed an eternity before the plane touched down in Vancouver. As I came down the stairs I wondered how I would recognize Joe, my cousin, who was waiting for me. I needn't have worried – someone was waving a little Austrian flag. It was him. He really did exist! Sometimes I had doubted his existence – this legendary cousin.

His whole family was there – his wife, daughters and son. He was no longer the lively young man his aunt had described. He had been I Canada a long time and his hair was graying. His face bears a resemblance to my father's, I thought. Although his mother had been sure he was unhappy in this country he certainly didn't look it. He looked, in fact, quite happy and content. "I think he likes it in Canada," I whispered to myself.

They had a nice big car and we drove through the city to their home. With a population of one hundred and sixty thousand in 1952, Vancouver was a different kind of city than Toronto – not as bubbly and cosmopolitan – but surrounded by mountains and ocean. It seemed to me to be a very nice place indeed.

Joe and his family made me feel at home – and a lovely home they had. I had my own room and Kurt was expected for the weekend from Kitimat. We talked and talked about relatives, wars, did Joe's mother have grey hair? Did his father still drink too much and did his sister still sing in the church? The kids wanted to know what teenagers wore in Europe. One thing I was sure they didn't wear – socks in winter. They wore long stockings and boots.

The next morning they all went their various ways – the children to school, Joe to work and Else to do some shopping. As Vivian was still sleeping and I was alone, I decided to write a few letters and send some pictures to my mother. I had already given them my address so my letters from them should arrive here at Joe's.

I was just settling down with pen and paper when the phone rang. I answered it, and felt grim foreboding as the operator announced "Austria calling."

Kurt's father had passed away.

How was I going to tell him? Should I call him in Kitimat? The funeral was already over. I decided therefore to wait until Kurt arrived at the weekend and then tell him.

I was glad when the baby started to cry and distracted my brooding. Else came back from shopping; when I gave her the news, she tried to comfort me, recalling how she had felt when her own father had passed away.

We all have to go through it – some sooner, some later.

Kurt came home on the weekend, and he took the news of his father's death with remarkable stoicism. Yet I was glad the baby's demands kept us busy. We have to keep going; and there was a new life in the cradle, stretching out her arms as if to comfort us.

Chapter Seven

A Return To The Mountains

Time kept ticking away. Kurt came to Vancouver once a month while I was waiting for available housing in Kemano. Finally we were told the company would not have accommodation for families, so Kurt transferred to Vancouver, to an office job. He had a good salary and we rented our first home. This was beyond our wildest expectations – our own home – even if it was only rented. We had many new friends, and now it was our turn to invite them to our own place. Amongst our friends was an Englishman, Len and his wife Mary. Len worked with Kurt in the office and he and his wife were often our guests. He liked Austrian cooking, but also was obsessed with learning to ski. And here I thought Englishmen all played golf!

In 1953, not many people skied for recreation. On the slopes of Grouse or Seymour Mountains, the languages spoken were most often German, Austrian or Scandinavian. But with the mountains so close, Kurt came down with a bad case of ski fever again, and bought himself a pair of skis. I accompanied him sometimes, but with the baby it was a bit difficult. We had to hike up to the top of Seymour Mountain in our heavy sealskins, and ski down. But Kurt's enthusiasm was contagious, and soon both Vivian and I were trudging up the mountain on weekends; or she would join her friends at the Teddy Bear Club and Kurt and I would go alone.

The Teddy Bear Club was a babysitting service run by two ladies. They had rented a cabin on the side of the mountain, furnished it with cribs, high chairs, toys, and all the things needed for babies and young children. For a small fee, the children could be left in their care while the parents skied.

We had marvelous times on the slopes and made so many friends there, among them Ushi and Erhardt, who where originally from Germany. Erhardt did not ski, as he had injured his leg during the war when he bailed out of a burning plane. Even though they did not ski, they loved to go up the mountain for the fresh air and just observe the activity. Ushi had two girls of her own, and would occasionally babysit Vivian while I learned to ski again. As one of her girls was Vivian's age, the children all played well together.

I particularly remember one New Year's Eve. We had all had a long, hard day's skiing and at the end of it there were bodies lying everywhere in the snow, too tired to ski, too tired even to get up. Our English friend, Len, had fallen into a hole in the snow and it took some time to get him out. (Undaunted, he was there the next Sunday, and the one after that, and so were we).

For my part, my skiing was not improving that much, but I was having fun, and I was no longer afraid to put on skis. "Oh, Mama, if you could see me now!"

Then came an enforced respite from skiing – I was pregnant again. This pregnancy would be easier emotionally, as our financial position had improved considerably. We were thinking of buying a house before the baby came. With all this excitement, I wrote home saying, "Dear Mama, I am going to have another house and baby." When their reply eventually came, they apparently thought I'd gone crazy.

•••

We really did it! We bought our first house and were in the process of moving when our baby was born – a boy this time, to be named Kurt Jr. Now our family was complete, and with both a son and a daughter we considered ourselves the happiest and luckiest people in the world.

•••

Kurt was getting ahead in our adopted country. He became a partner in a construction company, and studied English at night school (though he never lost his heavy accent; at our home we tried to speak both languages, and the children learned to speak German very well).

Our first Christmas in our new home was very exciting. Santa Claus came on the twenty-forth of December as he had in Austria – we kept that tradition. There were a lot of toys under the tree, and among them a tiny pair of skis for Vivian. Kurt Jr. was still to young. Had he been born in Austria, I joked, he would have received skis in the cradle, but our children were born in Canada.

Vivian was very happy with her skis and had to try them out in the back yard immediately! I wondered if she would become a ski fanatic as her father was.

Over the holidays we traveled to Mount Baker in Washington State, having heard that the skiing facilities were excellent. We rented a room in the hotel on top of the mountain. Though we had to get a special visa to travel to the United States, as we did not have our Canadian citizenship yet, we did have our own car, and the trip was very pleasant. The hotel was old, but nice and warm.

We took the children to the bunny hill, where Daddy gave his little girl her first skiing lessons. She showed more promise than I had, and her father was very, very proud. Kurt Jr. and I were content to leave them to it while we played about in the snow.

On our way home, there was a long line-up at the border, and when it came our turn to pass the customs official asked us to open our car's trunk. As the lock had frozen, this was impossible, but the inspector was determined now to see what that trunk contained! He called for hot water and went to no end of trouble to get that trunk open. Can you imagine his disappointment at finding nothing more contraband than wet ski clothes and boots? We wondered if our accents had made him so tenacious.

The pattern of our life that winter was to work hard all week, then each weekend strap the skis to the car and head for the mountains. We made many trips to Mount Baker, sometimes with friends. The incident with the frozen trunk lock had not deterred us from the fine skiing to be had there! This pattern was interrupted only when the children came down with measles and later with mumps.

As spring came, our attention turned from the hills to the garden, and we worked at clearing stumps and rocks from our land. It was hard work, but the results made it worthwhile.

One afternoon while we were working in the garden, Vivian announced that she would like a tree house. Her father, unable to refuse her slightest wish, sat down then and there and drew up plans. He promised it would be ready for her birthday. So Vivian, after a big hug and kiss for her doting dad, ran off to tell her brother. Little Kurt figured that if his sister was getting her wish, perhaps this was the right time to ask for what he wanted – a dog.

When the tree house was finished, it was a real masterpiece: a Hansel and Gretel cottage sitting between two trees, with real windows and a door. It was the envy of all the kids in the neighbourhood. Even little brother liked it, but Vivian left no doubt in his mind that it was her tree house! All pangs of jealousy disappeared when Kurt Jr. got his dog on his birthday – a white Samoyed we named Snowball. All the children had fun with Snowball, and the tree house became a regular meeting place for the neighbourhood children.

But a tree house and a dog weren't quite enough; now it was "Mom, can we have a cat?" How could I say no, especially when the neighbour was giving them away free? I couldn't even claim they were too expensive!

"Oh well, I suppose no family is complete without a dog and cat. All right, go and get it." Joy reigned!

Occasionally now, Kurt's work took him out of town, and at these times I was glad to have a dog around the house.

Sometimes we would accompany Kurt to Prince George or Prince Rupert, and it was interesting to see the country and get to know its people. On one of these trips, we traveled to an area near Williams Lake and met some Native families; in fact, some of the men worked for Kurt. This was my first contact with First Nations people, and they reminded me of our Gypsies at home. They were friendly but aloof, although it wasn't long before Vivian and Kurt Jr. were happily playing with the Indian children. We met one very interesting couple on this trip. She was schoolteacher from Switzerland and he was a full-blooded Indian. They had married and had the most beautiful children.

Kurt had always wanted to own his own construction company. I knew that with his incredible determination and strength it would not take too long for him to achieve this goal. His was the personality that could come to a strange country and build a new and successful life. His brother, on the other hand, would probably have turned back the second day – he was more gentle and afraid to take a risk. But once Kurt started something, he had to finish it.

I had not such determination. Although I loved Canada, part of my heart was still back home. Some of my friends advised me to go back to Austria for a visit, and then on my return I would feel more "at home" here. It seemed like a good idea.

As Kurt had neither the time nor the desire to go back to Austria, I began making plans to travel there with the children. Everything was organized, my passport in order, and I had even bought a new suitcase when Kurt arrived home to tell me I had to postpone my trip. An opportunity had arisen for him to buy out his partner and be sole owner of his own contracting firm! I was glad he'd be living his dreams, but disappointed to delay mine. The hardest part was writing home – I had been promising a visit "next year" for quite some years already.

•••

Kurt's business was proceeding with great speed and vigour to become a flourishing enterprise. There was no stopping Kurt's drive for success, though I did wish he'd slow down a bit, and not smoke so many cigarettes – I was concerned for his health. But as long as he could ski on weekends, Kurt was happy; if he couldn't, he was miserable. The children enjoyed spending the weekends on the slopes too, but occasionally Kurt would go alone and the children and I would go the park.

And one Sunday, as we were strolling through Stanley Park, I noticed a couple who kept looking in our direction and then talking together, then looking again. As we drew closer to them I recognized – Maria and Willie from the ship! Of course – they had come to Vancouver originally. We sat down on one of the benches and talked until dark. We exchanged addresses, and I could hardly wait to tell Kurt about it.

"Guess who I bumped into today?"

A day on the slopes had left him too tired for guessing games, so I told him. Of course he remembered Maria and Willie and was glad to hear the news – what they were doing now, that they had their own house, were doing well, and loved it here.

Like Kurt, Maria and Willie had discovered that noting was given free; but opportunities were available for those willing to find them, just as we had to find those little Austrian restaurants on Robsonstrasse, and discover the Heidleberg German restaurant. Any Sunday afternoon would see a lot of homesick people eating their bratwurst and sauerkraut, while they listened to *Lili Marlene* or some other *Schmazig Musik*. Our own preference was the Johann Strauss Café – they also had dancing in the evening. Where else but Canada could you dance to the tunes of Johann Strauss played by a Hungarian musician, while being served beer by a French waitress and food cooked by Chinese! Isn't it great!

•••

Another year was ending – and what better place to welcome in the New Year than the Johann Strauss? What a mixture of people were there, though the majority were from Austria or Germany. Many of them had already obtained their Canadian Citizenship papers.

That was our goal for this New Year, 1956 – to become Canadian citizens! The day of our hearing was like a graduation day, with all the excitement, the butterfly stomach, the nervousness of schoolchildren.

That morning as we dressed, Kurt and I quizzed each other from the pamphlets we had been studying; Kurt cool as ever and I so anxious:

"Where are the parliament buildings?"

"Toronto," said Kurt.

"Wrong – Ottawa."

"How many provinces are there?" We both knew that one – it happens to be the same in Austria.

"When was the British North America act passed?" We both had to look in the book again – 1867."

"What is the function of the Lieutenant Governor?"

"He is the official representative of Her Majesty, The Queen," answered a loud voice behind us. It was our good friend Dough, who had just arrived and who would do us the honour of being our witness for this ceremony.

As we continued getting ready he thumbed through the booklets and admitted that he didn't know all the answers himself. He suggested that if we didn't know the answer to a particular question, we should just smile – he was sure we would not be refused citizenship!

We arrived at the Court House just in time – everyone else was already seated. We recognized a few people from the Anna Salen, our old ship, all waiting for their diploma. Since our name was Baumkirschner, I thought, we would be one of the first to be called – if they proceeded alphabetically.

"Don't worry so much," Doug kept saying. "If you don't make it this time, you will next time."

Kurt just smiled. I envied his confidence – I had studied twice as hard as he had, and my English was much better, yet I was twice as nervous as he. He just had no right to be so calm!"

He just went on smiling – all the way up to the front when they called his name and he was still smiling when he came back – he had made it!

Then it was my turn. They asked me a few questions, one of which I thought was inane – they asked me how I liked Canada. If I hated the place, would I be standing here?

Then we sang our new song, O Canada, and, with scrolls in hand, were ready to leave. We had to celebrate, and as we drove to the restaurant I read the letter from the Minister of Citizenship and Immigration, Ellen L Fairclough:

Dear Madam:

I wish to take this opportunity of congratulating you personally upon the attainment of Canadian Citizenship. By this certificate of citizenship you have been granted the rights and privileges of a citizen in Canada. These rights and privileges entitle you to freedom of speech, religion, thought and action, the right to vote as you choose, and the right to be secure in your possessions.

Your citizenship carries with it the obligation of defending your adopted country in time of need, of living in peaceful brotherhood with your fellow Canadians, (So you had better be good to me, now, Doug interjected), *and of doing your part in the preservation of Canadian ideals and institutions.*

I extend to you a warm welcome on this solemn occasion and I invite you to share with us the ancient liberties of a free people living together in harmony, under a democratic government which recognizes the rights of all its citizens.

There it was! It certainly gave one a proud feeling! We had by this time reached our destination – the Johann Strauss of course! Where else could we celebrate, but at the restaurant where we had made our New Year's resolve to achieve what we had this day!

There were a lot of new Canadians there, also celebrating. We thought everyone at the Court House had been accepted, but found there were a few rejections. One Italian did not understand the question the Judge had asked him, so was told he'd better brush up on his English.

"By the way, Kurt," inquired Doug, "What did the Judge ask you?"

Taking another fierce puff on his cigarette, Kurt replied, "He asked me if I knew any good Austrian restaurants." I wonder!

"You know the first thing I'm going to do as a new citizen – I'm going to exercise my rights by not cleaning Kurt's shoes anymore – nor the windows. I was told by some Canadian girls that that's how it's done here!"

Kurt had his answer ready. "She just wants to adopt the good things."

But of course – don't we all?

The waiter brought us a bottle of Sylvaner.

"Well, here's to you, Canada!"

The next day I was telling everyone I met about my citizenship, including my Chinese friend, Mable. She invited me to a Chinese restaurant right in the heart of Chinatown by way of celebrating. I had been to Chinatown before, and had loved Chinese food from the moment I tasted it. But it was quite different to visit with someone who was actually Chinese – even the food was prepared differently for us.

While we were eating, I plied Mabel with questions about some paintings and figurines and about China generally. After all, it was in British Columbia where I first came into contact with Chinese people.

When I first told her about my citizenship, she had said, "Aren't you lucky!"

"What do you mean? Don't you have yours?"

"Oh, yes, I have it now. But my parents were denied theirs for a long time, and in fact they couldn't vote until 1947."

"Why was that?"

And so she told me the story of the Chinese in Canada.

Many Chinese found work on the railway. All that rail through the perilous Fraser Canyon was laid mostly by Chinese labourers, who worked for very little pay, no priviledges, and not enough money to go home.

My lunch was getting cold as I listened, fascinated, to the contribution her countrymen had made to this new land.

The waiter brought us tea, and soon afterward we left the restaurant and browsed a bit through the Chinese shops. On the way home we stopped for a minute on Robsonstrasse for a little-minute shopping; it was like traveling from China to Vienna or Munich in the space of a few city blocks! And so, after a quick look into the European News shop for the latest German papers, we hurried home to avoid rush hour.

●●●

Summer was coming to an end and it was time to ready the Christmas parcels for Europe. I was so happy that I could now afford to send gifts, as they were still struggling back home. We were still not so very well off financially, so I frequented rummage sales, as much for the fun of them as for the bargains I could pick up. This would be another Christmas when my parcel would have to compensate for my absence.

It's a very sentimental time, Christmas, especially as the universal carols, "Silent Night" and "O Tannenbaum" fill the air. So many memories of Christmas as it was! But the traditions of times past were changing; we had traditionally opened our parcels from home and our family gifts on Christmas Eve, as is done in Austria, but this year Vivian pleaded for Christmas morning, the same as all her Canadian friends. But one thing I refused to change: "I will never go out on Christmas eve!"

Our traditional Christmas tree underwent a few changes, too. "Mummy, why is the tree so white?" asked a little voice.

"White? But it's green!"

"Yes, but next door their tree is so colourful."

So we added a little colour. So now we had not only Canadian Citizenship, but also a Canadian Christmas tree. "I must admit I like white, gold and silver better, and I'm sure I'll get used to it."

We opened our parcels on Christmas morning as Vivian had asked, and found all the traditional gifts – candles, walnuts and *Mozartkugel* from Salzburg – the only place that really knows how to make them. And then, a surprise. A record. I put it on the record player; first we heard bells ringing, then a voice: my brother Fritz, wishing us a Merry Christmas and hoping to see us soon! Then he started to sing. He didn't have a beautiful voice, but to me it was the most beautiful gift we received. It was as well that the children with their toys provided a diversion or I would have been lost in memories that day.

CHAPTER EIGHT
HOMEWARD BOUND

I had postponed my trip to Austria another year, and then another, and it was not until I received word that my father was not too well (he was close to eighty years old by this time) that we decided I'd best make the trip especially since the children could still go for half-fare.

We booked our flight for June, and I started collecting Canadian gifts to take along – a toy black bear for my mother-in-law, some totem poles, Indian dolls and even a pressed Dogwood leaf. We had a most beautiful Dogwood tree in our garden, and there are no trees like it in Austria, nor perhaps in all of Europe.

Everything proceeded on schedule except my nerves, which were playing their usual tricks. I supposed it was normal to feel so jittery when returning home for the first time. I had left with Kurt, and here I was with two little Canadians, who were very excited about going on a big plane. While I was packing, the radio was very appropriately playing: *Fly the Ocean with a Silver Plane.* Each of the children had their own little suit-case, though I worried about how far they would carry them. However, I was assured that there was always help available for young mothers.

Pour good-byes to Daddy were tearful, but he cheered Vivian by saying that he might come over later, and that she would have one grandfather and two grandmothers when she got there.

We secured a window seat and stayed glued to the porthole as long as we could. At last the sign flashed "Fasten Seat Belts" and up we went. Vancouver shrank into the distance, and so did the lonely figure we were leaving behind.

We were served drinks and supper, as it was an evening flight, and I had hoped that after the meal the children would be sleepy. But the stewardess and I had our hands full, as Vivian got sick and little Kurt had earaches. How I wished big Kurt were there! But finally sleep came for the little ones, and I was left with my thoughts and memories: that first time we talked about going to Canada; our wedding; my mother clasping my hand and running alongside the train that would carry us so far away, for so long.

I reflected on how much I missed my family and supposed they missed me, too, every bit as much. And now I lived as a part of two different worlds – or were they so very different? I would know when I was once again "home" in Austria. I missed many things, but on the other hand I had enjoyed so many new things, too.

Outside the aeroplane it was dark, without stars or moon, and I wondered what Kurt was doing, and what they were doing in Salzburg. I must have dozed because I suddenly jolted to consciousness of a child crying – not mine, thank goodness! And then it was daybreak, and I knew we were not far from Amsterdam, where we were to change planes for Munich.

I had never been to Amsterdam before; in fact it suddenly struck me that I hardly knew Europe, and it would be exciting to come to know it a little better.

Then the announcement that we would soon be landing, and all those nice quiet people became pushers, and shovers and elbowers getting ready to de-plane. Everyone wanted to be first. No one was meeting me in Amsterdam, but there was help for me with the children anyway. I was what they called a "green" passenger – my first transatlantic flight. I was annoyed at being so helpless, but for everyone there is a first time, a time of learning.

We had to wait for our connection to Munich, so had time to look around. It was a little difficult to sightsee with two small children, so we decided to sit and do some people watching. There were Italians, talking with extravagant gestures, French almost singing when they spoke, Austrians and Germans usually very loud and a little more round in the middle, and the British with their usual self-assurance. Put them all in a bag, I thought, shake well and you have Canadians.

Our flight was announced, and shortly we were en route for Munich, I with butterflies in my stomach. It seemed I was as nervous coming home as I had been when leaving, so many years ago.

This flight was a short one, and the pushing and shoving again. So unlike Canada, where they automatically line up for buses or trains.

And there was everyone to greet us – my mamma and papa, my brother, Fritz, and his wife and two children – everyone except my father-in-law. I was momentarily shocked at how old they all looked. Then I was engulfed in kisses, hugs, tears and laughter, and we were escorted to two waiting cars for the trip to Salzburg. It was a two-hour drive to Salzburg on the Autobahn, but we had so much to talk about that the time passed very quickly.

We stayed in the hotel where my father worked, since there was still not enough accommodation for all the refugees. Our families were still considered refugees, as they had not been born in Salzburg or the Land of Salzburg. In spite of the ruins and scars left by the war, I had a very special feeling about being back again – a feeling as warm and comfortable as my bed in the hotel. There was even a chamber pot in the night-table: Salzburg, and Austria, does not bend easily to progress. Skyscrapers were not allowed, but somehow one had sneaked in and looked very out-of-place. With so much to see and do, we needed that good night's sleep.

When Kurt Jr. wakened me in the morning, I opened the windows and heard bells ringing all over the city. Of course, it was Sunday morning! I realized then how I had missed those church bells in Canada. My father was walking up and down the street in front of the hotel as if he owned it. That had always been his dearest wish – to own his own hotel. He was so old now, and still had no capital – I wished I could have helped him.

We had all planned to meet for lunch downstairs. Lunch in Salzburg is a celebration. People there start work at 8:00 in the morning, and work until 5:00 or 5:30, but they have a two-hour lunch break each day. They do enjoy their food, and so did I! Kurt Jr. wasn't happy at all – he wanted a peanut butter and steak sandwich!

We had made arrangements to go to Italy for fourteen days and take my mother with us. Neither she nor I had ever been to Italy and were looking forward to seeing Venice.

Italy was lovely – and hot. We went swimming every day in the Adriatic Sea, which is very salty, and emerged with salt crusting our bodies. My mother went wading, as she didn't swim; she was in good company, for the beach was covered with tanned bodies soaking up the sun. I noticed that my mother's bathing suit lacked a prosthesis, which she needed since that long-ago operation for breast cancer, and made a mental note to send her a new bathing suit from Canada.

We walked a lot, and it wasn't Mamma, but the children who tired. The children enjoyed the glass factories, especially when they each were given a glass horse, which they had watched being made. I was fascinated by the jewellery shops and the fantastic work of the goldsmiths – like tiny spiders and flies all made out of gold.

On the day we left Italy I could just close the zipper on my slacks. Oh, that Italian pasta – I ate it morning, noon and night!

Back again in Salzburg, we did more sightseeing. We took a horse and buggy ride (the children loved it) past beautiful churches and castles. I pointed out to them where their Dad used to work, and the driver pointed out where Mozart was born. I searched the faces in the crowds in vain for an old friend or a remembered countenance.

There was the Café Bazar where Kurt had told me the story of his capture by the Russians; for old times, I would go there the following day and have coffee and *kuchen* (I remembered those three pieces of delicious cake)! I would also take the children to the Marionnetten Theatre and to the Catacombs. The days were flying by and we had to hurry if we wanted to see everything.

On our last evening everyone was giving me advice on how to behave and what to see in Paris. We had booked our flight to Canada via Paris, as I had always dreamed of going to the City of Light. My papa had lived and worked in Paris many years ago. He spoke French fluently and I wished I could have taken him with me. I promised to phone from Paris, and also to write.

It was time to say goodbye to my family again, but this time it was a different leave-taking. This time, I had another home waiting for me at the end of a much shortened journey, and two little people at my side who would give me all the love I might miss. *Au Revoir! Auf Wiedersetien!* Goodbye! I could see them wiping their tears as I looked out the plane's widow; they could not see mine.

● ● ●

Our trip to Paris was by no means uneventful. We were to change planes in Zurich, but the plane which was to take us to Paris developed engine trouble, and the airline requested that all those whose trip to Paris was not essential to please postpone or cancel it. I was advised, especially since I had the children with me, to cancel my sightseeing trip to Paris and fly directly home to Canada. To be so close to Paris – my lifelong dream—and then have to give it up! I just couldn't; so at midnight our plane left Zurich for Paris carrying mostly diplomats, me and my two children!

Vivian and Kurt slept all the way to Paris, and I longed for someone to talk to and share my romantic thoughts and feelings on coming to Paris. The plane set down very gently, as though wishing not to awaken anyone who was sleeping. But to me this was no time to sleep. This was Paris – alive and awake!

Tucking one sleeping child under one arm and taking flight bag and other child's had, I joined the long line-up for taxis. I was saved by a benevolent gendarme who pulled me out of the line and packed me into the next waiting taxi. After much hunting around our driver finally found our hotel, and after I had put the two children to bed, I opened the widow to gaze out on the Paris night. It was raining!

There was a knock at the door; the old proprietor asked if there was anything I needed. "Yes, a bottle of champagne – I must greet Paris tonight!"

The next morning, after an early breakfast, we went to the Eiffel Tower, and the Notre Dame cathedral. The cathedral was awe – and prayer – inspiring. Kurt Jr. asked, "Do you have to pray in French here?" I assured him that God understands all languages.

And finally, it was time to go back to Canada. The children were longing for a hamburger at the White Spot; and Daddy would be waiting for us at the Vancouver Airport. Our holiday was over; the old routine of work and school beckoned.

CHAPTER TEN

A VISIT FROM KURT'S MOTHER

School had become a little more serious for Kurt and Vivian, with competition between them to excel. During the week, work at school or office, house and garden kept us busy, but again the weekends were for skiing. We still went up Seymour and Grouse Mountains and, occasionally to Mount Baker. One Easter holiday we went to Sun Valley, Colorado – it was the "in" spot at the time. Among the V.I.P.s skiing there that week were Jacqueline Kennedy with her children and Robert Kennedy and his family.

Of course, we didn't stay at the chalet – we couldn't afford it – but we found a very nice place in Ketchum, a little farther away from the slopes. We didn't mind the walk – who needs the chalet when we had powder snow! It was like magic; I was actually skiing! Kurt couldn't believe his eyes as I sailed all the way down the run through the knee-deep powder, without a tumble or falter. It was marvelous!

Evenings were always fun, too, discovering all sorts of new restaurants. Kurt always preferred Austrian, Czechoslovakian or Hungarian food – *"Alt Wiener kueche."* We all enjoyed the wiener schnitzel and Hungarian goulash, but Kurt Jr. preferred steak – he could eat it morning, noon and night. His father abhorred steak!

However, once on the ski slopes there was no disagreement – just everyone trying their best, and that pleased Kurt, who, of course, out-skied us all.

Some men like to watch football games, others like to play golf, but for Kurt the passion was skiing, and I knew from the first that either I could go along with this love, or I could get a divorce!

•••

Life had resolved into a comfortable routine, punctuated by regular familial histrionics to dispel any threat of boredom.

Vivian was now approaching her teens, and when she was not usurping the bathroom, to the chagrin of her little brother, she was threatening to cut off the beautiful red-blonde hair which cascaded almost to her waist and formed a perfect backdrop for her grey-green eyes.

Our Samoyed, Snowball, had developed diabetes and so required an insulin injection every morning, the administration of which fell to me. Though difficult at first, Snowball soon adapted, as she knew the needle was always followed by breakfast.

One particular morning, after the injection, the breakfast and sending off the various family members on their various ways, I looked for the cat to give her the left-over milk. After a good deal of searching I found her under Kurt, Jr.'s bed, acting very peculiarly. A quick trip to the veterinarian produced the diagnosis – leukemia! After a telephone consultation with Kurt it was decided to have the poor beast put to sleep; and in spite of Kurt's moral support, I found myself crying on the way home over the loss. I dreaded the reaction of the children, as they both loved their cat. And indeed, dread was well-founded, for there was much weeping and screaming before they finally went to bed, partially-consoled by the promise of another cat and the idea of a symbolic burial for Brownie beneath the tree house.

That tree house was still popular, though not as picturesque as it had been. Originally it had sat between two trees, but one of these had been blown down during Typhoon Frieda, leaving just a stump. Still, it was a child's refuge from an adult world. In fact, one morning as I went out to give the children a piece of news, I saw a smoke rising from the tree house. Thinking the building was of fire, I ran towards it, bursting in on some very embarrassed youngsters experimenting with their first cigarette!

The news I was bearing, on that occasion, had to do with a letter we had received some time earlier from Kurt's mother, who was so very lonely since Kurt's father had passed away. With all her children some distance from her. She was all alone and we agreed to arrange to have her come visit us awhile in Canada -- much cheaper than flying our whole family to Salzburg! And so on that particular morning of the tree house "fire", we had received word that she would indeed be visiting us around Dominion Day. What fun to get ready for Grandmother's visit! The spare room received a new blanket and pillow; we planted lots of flowers in the garden, and everything indoors and out was polished to a high shine. And then it was Dominion Day, and we were off to the airport to greet our first visitor from the old country.

I was very excited, and even Kurt, pacing up and down, puffing on a cigarette, was perhaps a little less calm than usual. And then – there she was! You couldn't miss her – her skirt was a little too long by our fashions, her hair a little too straight, and she wore no makeup – but nevertheless, this was a very regal-looking lady. The children were soon being kissed and hugged, whether they liked it or not!

I could hardly wait to get her home and see what she would say about our house. She was certainly impressed by our Mercedes Benz, and by the city –she asked questions all the way home. And when we got home, she put down her handbag and wandered around the house, inspecting everything. She was very proud of her son and his family!

Kurt's business took him to Prince George, as his firm was doing some building in Smithers, and as it was school vacation, we decided to travel along with him and show Grandmother some of the North Country. We hadn't seen too much of it ourselves, so it would be an interesting trip for all concerned. And while there, we could visit Ushi and Erhardt, our very good friends, who had just moved up there.

We talked constantly while en route. Grandmother wanted to know about everything we saw; the trouble was, we didn't know all the answers! Sometimes the children came to the rescue when the questions were historical or geographical; their German was good enough that they could converse with Grandma, who was delighted that her grandchildren spoke German.

We watched a black bear cross the road on day – a little too late for us to take a picture, but a thrill nevertheless, especially for Grandma, who had never seen a bear before. Nor had she seen all the different kinds of West Coast birds – she made a note of them – and noted too that the birds' forest habitat was much denser than the forests back home. She said it would be no fun getting lost in those woods!

We drove miles and miles, with a detour to show Grandmother Barkerville, a restored ghost town relic of the Klondike gold rush. We took rolls and rolls of pictures, including some finally, of the bears we met.

One week after our departure from Vancouver, we arrived in Prince George, around noon and our friends Ushi and Erhardt had lunch waiting for us. Their house was situated in the forest overlooking a river. It reminded us of scenes described by Ganghofer, an Austrian author who wrote of such settings.

While Ushi drove us around Prince George (a typical northern town) Kurt finished his business and then he and Erhardt went fishing, a sport they both enjoyed.

The weather was very hot, so while the men were fishing the rest of us went swimming, Grandmother repeating that the country was just like Austria, only bigger.

On our return trip we took a slightly different route, and encountered a back of rain clouds. The nearer we got to Vancouver, the harder the rain came down!

All too soon, Grandmother's visit with us ended. She was going on to visit Kurt's sister, who lived in Delaware. Our request that she stay with us permanently was turned down graciously, for she missed the familiar home and shops and friends of Austria. Still, when we drove her out to the airport she was loaded down with gifts and things she had bought for herself, including a couple of doughnuts – she dearly loved those Canadian doughnuts!

CHAPTER ELEVEN
THE SOUND OF MUSIC.

Kurt was working very hard, and business was good. He seemed to be building schools everywhere! When I asked him why so many schools were needed, he replied that in Canada each school has five bathrooms for each classroom, whereas in Austria there are five classrooms for one bathroom.

In fact, Kurt was doing well enough in his business to surprise us one day with his announced promise to build us a swimming pool. I thought, "I suppose I will have to take my laundry line down – the neighbors will be glad. A clothesline in such an exclusive area is unthinkable! But to me it makes no sense to put the laundry in a dryer when it's seventy degrees outside. Besides, clothes smell so much better when dried outdoors."

When the pool was completed, we of course invited all our friends over for an inaugural swim. That summer the pool became the center of activity, and the treehouse was neglected – as was Snowball, our dog, who was quite upset at this turn of events! I stood watching the neighborhood children splashing about, and surveyed the beautiful yard and house which I called home. If only Mrs. Drachmann, my first Canadian employer, could see me now! Perhaps my house didn't have twenty rooms, but it was a lovely home, and had a lovely garden. We had worked hard for our place in the sun, especially Kurt, whose workday began at 7 am or, if he were traveling to an out-of-town building site, he'd be on the road at 5 am or earlier.

•••

The opera was coming to town, and I decided it was time to introduce Vivian to it. As Kurt didn't care for opera, I invited Vivian's friend Kenny and his mother to accompany us to the opening night performance. And what a treat to see Vivian, who usually preferred her blue jeans, actually enjoying getting all dressed up for this outing. Of course, we intended to include late dinner after the show!

The opera was *Lucia di Lammermoor*, introducing soprano Joan Sutherland to Vancouver audiences. While our party was thrilled by her voice, and by the opera itself, I'm afraid I embarrassed the others with my constant "Bravos."

That night, and that performance, inspired Vivian to become a singer, and she was serious enough to begin taking voice lessons. After that, whenever there was a play or musical at school, Vivian was in it.

One morning, as I walked to the mailbox, I had that old familiar feeling of foreboding. Sure enough, there was an airmail letter from home, which informed us that my father had cancer and an operation was indicated. My first thought was that he was too old for an operation of that kind. In fact, when I had last seen him, on our trip to Austria a few years before, he had looked very unwell and very old. In fact, he was much older that my mother. Oh, how I wished I could be there! But there were many things occupying my thoughts as the time for the operation drew near.

There was that morning we spent vainly looking for Snowball so the children could give him his customary petting before they set off for school. After much calling there was still no sign of him, and as time was fleeting, I decided to drive the kids to school. On my way home, I found snowball lying in a ditch, very sick. The vet could not help him; apparently he had eaten something that had been poisoned, and died in agony as a result.

It was a terrible shock to all the family. Kurt Jr. was the first one home, the first one told; he just dropped his books and walked out of the house. He didn't even return until after midnight, soaking wet from the inevitable rain. Vivian, meanwhile, had locked herself in her room and didn't come out until she heard Kurt Jr. come home. After Kurt had changed his clothes and had some warm food, we all went to bed very quietly, each with our own sorrowful thoughts for the little white bundle of fluff we had brought home so very many years ago, and whom we all would miss so much.

And so another New Year drew near. Some friends had invited us to welcome it with them at our favourite spot, the Johann Strauss Café. To go to the Johann Strauss was always a little like going home – they played our kind of music, and we always met old friends there. This year there was a new dance rage – The Twist – but since nobody had really mastered it, the orchestra soon switched back to the familiar polkas and waltzes. That was better!

At the party the talk naturally turned to skiing, and we decided, at someone's suggestion, to make a party to go to Mt. Hood, near Portland, Oregon and try out the snow there. By this time Vivian was old enough to care for her brother and so Kurt and I went by ourselves. Mount Hood was fabulous – not enough challenge for Kurt, but I loved it. The Dollar Run was just my speed, and the Million Dollar Castle in the clouds – Timberline Lodge – was just wonderful. I hated to leave, and promised myself that we would return soon.

Personally, I prefer walking in the snow to driving in the rain, but rain was all we had that winter in Vancouver. The grey skies matched my mood as I waited on my father's imminent operation.

And then the phone ringing in the middle of the night – Austria calling – I hardly heard the rest of it – poor old dad – how I wished he could have come to Canada to visit us – he spoke such perfect English – I must go home to see mother soon....

And we did fly back to Austria for a few hours. One night we saw the film *The Sound of Music*. Kurt had not been back to Austria since we first emigrated – Canada was a good place to live and we had settled in and were happy here. But *The Sound of Music* had been filmed in Salzburg, our old hometown and Kurt's birthplace; and when they sang *Edelweiss*, I noticed Kurt very busy with his handkerchief. I saw the movie five times, but for Kurt, once was enough.

Vivian and Kurt Jr. were teenagers now with summer jobs. Kurt Jr. helped his father in the office. His hair was a little longer now, and we secretly hoped he would soon visit the barber. But no – the Flower Children were in full bloom everywhere, in the streets, on the highways, and right in our own home. In the summer the girls wore long skirts and sandals, or went barefoot. The boys wore their hair long and usually had a guitar strapped on their backs, whether they could play it or not. Bewildered parents hoped it was just a summertime fad, but the trend continued for half a decade. Sometimes the young people were stoned out of their minds from drugs. What had happened to them? Why did they spurn their comfortable homes? Maybe all the wars, assassinations, nuclear weapons and moon flights scared the hell out of them! Meanwhile, we got used to the long hair and resigned ourselves to waiting out the craze.

•••

Another winter, and Kurt was still searching for the perfect mountain. We had heard rumours about Whistler mountain, which was supposed to have excellent skiing, good powder snow, and not much of a place yet... but all an avid skier needs is good snow. So Kurt was off to check out the rumours. When he returned from his Whistler expedition, he couldn't stop talking all through dinner about his new enthusiasm – he had found the perfect mountain! You'd think he owned the place! And so a new era had begun for our family: The Whistler phase.

CHAPTER TWELVE
THE WHISTLER PHASE BEGINS

The Squamish highway follows one of the most scenic routes in the world, though and extremely dangerous one, and we had driven the road many times. Beyond Squamish was at that time only a rough logging road, which we had ventured with some friends once, for a picnic outing. And once, we had skied on Garibaldi Mountain – it was a long hike up, and had but one rope-tow, so high that when a youngster was holding it and someone ahead of him let go, he flew up into the air! Those who missed the "snow –cat" had to ski down to base camp in its tracks, and on icy days it was anything but fun.

Whistler Mountain, the day I first saw it, looked forbidding. It rose to a height of seven thousand one hundred and eighteen feet – some five thousand feet above the valley. That first day it was foggy and the slopes were icy; I really didn't share Kurt's enthusiasm! The weather didn't faze Kurt – he just raved on about the mountain's excellence. In those days, the mountain didn't attract many skiers; the old logging road was not intended for winter driving and was extremely hazardous. But to a ski enthusiast, that was nothing – once on the mountain, the journey's risks were forgotten.

I chose to stay at the base most days, waiting for Kurt. There wasn't much to see or do, no place to have coffee, so I just wandered around. As always, the same types of people – a handful of Austrians and Norwegians – seemed to frequent the slopes. Franz Wilhelmson, who deserves much credit for the growth of Whistler, was often there; also Stefan, who had discovered Whistler a little earlier and had started the Tyrol Ski Club. He made beautiful carved furniture when he wasn't on the slopes. Stefan had lived at Whistler quite a long time already, and claimed he didn't ever wish to live anywhere else. We often saw him walking up the mountain with his skis, scorning the lifts.

There was no longer any question of where we would ski on weekends. The local sloped didn't have much snow that winter, and Whistler became our home away from home. It was the next best thing to the Alps, and was heavenly to European skiers.

Every time we went up to Whistler, we noticed changes. Some people were building A-frame cabins where they could stay for two or three days, to save the journey back and forth. Some even went so far as to decorate their window frames and paint them – it gave the place a Swiss or Austrian look.

We made many new friends, and, of course, when they opened the L'Aprés Cafeteria, we found them all there after skiing. There was Austrian jodelling, dancing and even Austrian beer – each week it was another Oktoberfest!

We met Stan and Midge – both avid skiers from England. Midge was a lovely person, kind and considerate, and because of her encouragement I began to ski the mountain regularly. Because she was originally from England, I felt I owed it to Mother Austria to go up there and try – it was the least I could do!

For my birthday, I had been given a new shiny blue ski outfit and I thought I would try it out. It was a good skiing day, lots of new snow, and I felt confident. I loved powder snow, thinking it wouldn't be so hard to land on if I fell! Four of us went up the mountain. Soon Kurt was well ahead, and Stan and Midge wanted to go for lunch. I wanted to have one more run before joining them, and sent them ahead.

While they were waiting in the roundhouse, I was coming down the mountain – on a stretcher. I had been run over by a two hundred pound male skier, and my leg was broken. The men of the Ski Patrol were fantastic – all bearded, so I called them the bearded angels. They just seemed to float down with me through terrain I could hardly have walked over. Thank God for the Ski Patrol!

Kurt, Midge, Stan and a few others came to see me in the First Aid room. When someone asked if I could ski again, Kurt answered that we simply had to get a better ski binding – the one I had didn't open up automatically.

•••

It was summer again, and I was thankful we could spend a little time at home. As we were cleaning up the garden one-day, we noticed that the tree house was really suffering neglect – besides bringing down one of its sheltering trees, Typhoon Frieda had made a few dents in it and the roof was a bit askew. Kurt decided to fix it up and put on a new roof. It was a hot day, but he was determined to finish it, he didn't ask for help, nor did he want it. Toward the evening it began to rain, but Kurt still worked on the tree house roof.

When he finally came in, his face was a terrible colour, and, frightened, I decided to call the doctor. Our family doctor was a countryman from Vienna who also loved skiing, and Kurt and he had become good friends over the years. He didn't live far from us, and came over immediately. He confirmed my own suspicion – heart attack. Said aloud, the words sent chills down my spine. He left some pills and said that if Kurt didn't show any improvement, the ambulance was to be called. He called the condition angina pectoris, and after he left I checked the encyclopedia to research the condition. Slamming the volume closed, I immediately called an ambulance and within an hour Kurt was in the intensive care unit. Later, moved to his own private room, incorrigible Kurt conducted his business from his hospital bed – there was just no stopping him!

•••

On his return home, Kurt told us that he had decided he was going back to Austria for a visit, and I was going with him. It would be his first visit home since we came to Canada, and I was sure his mother would be glad to see him. I was also looking forward to seeing my mother and brothers again. We arranged for our old friends from the refugee boat, Maria and Willy, to stay at our house and look after things. Vivian and Kurt were no longer children, but this arrangement made us feel easier about leaving them.

We wrote to Austria to tell the family we were coming, and then planned our itinerary: London, Paris, Amsterdam and a few other places we had not seen before.

London was foggy – no surprise to me; I remembered my father's tales of London fogs. We visited Windsor Castle, the Tower of London and other landmarks, but I was anxious for the next stop on our schedule.

Paris! How I loved that city! This time I really saw it all – shopping on the Champs Elysees – sitting at sidewalk cafes watching the rest of the world go by! In the evening we made a tour of the nightclubs and then on to the Moulin Rouge, where I almost expected to meet the ghost of Toulouse-Lautrec.

Our hotel was centrally located, and we wandered around finding gifts to take with us. "Oh, I could stay here forever!" On the last day I decided to go to a beauty parlour, and Kurt decided he needed a haircut too. The desk clerk suggested a place nearby which could accommodate us both. When we met after our sessions with the scissors, I hardly recognized my husband. What had they done to him? Where were all his curls? He told me he didn't know the French word for "stop," so they just went on cutting!

The flight to Austria was pleasant, but I giggled every time I looked at Kurt – you'd think he was in the army!

Hair or no hair, him mother was quite overwhelmed at seeing him again. And there were all of my family – all except my mother. The look on my brother's face braced me for the news: my mother was in hospital and was scheduled for an operation the next day, for cancer of the liver. So, while Kurt and his mother went to Graz to visit his brother, I spent my time at the hospital with my mother.

She had been a beautiful woman – dark hair and green eyes, but now she was so thin, and her hearing was very poor: everyone in the room listened to our conversations. The doctors held out little hope of recovery; I remembered back twenty-five years, to when she'd had her left breast removed during the air raid. But now, they said, there was nothing anyone could do. I spent most of my time at her bedside, combing her hair, holding her hand, remembering the many times in the past she had held mine to comfort me.

Occasionally Kurt and I would go out to dinner or a show with my brothers, but there was no joy in these excursions for me.

I was debating whether to stay with my mother until the end, when the decision was made for me. We had a letter from Kurt Jr., saying that he was dropping out of school and taking a job. I knew I had to go back to Canada!

The plane seemed to take forever getting us back to Canada, but when we finally got back home, we quickly sorted everything out. Kurt Jr. not only continued in school, he even got his hair cut! Some of his friends had their hair cut, too. Now where had all the flower children gone? Perhaps they went south for the winter.

We had been back only a few days, and I was still sorting things out, terrified every time the telephone rang and anxious for word of my mother's condition. And then the call came, and the news was delivered by my brother in a broken voice. I couldn't believe the end had come so quickly. Only a few days! I felt so badly that I hadn't stayed those few extra days; and the chance was lost, I couldn't go back again. All I could do was send flowers. And suddenly I felt like an orphan, having no father and no mother any more.

CHAPTER THIRTEEN

EDELWEISS VILLAGE

Kurt had completely recovered from his heart attack by winter, and was allowed to go skiing again. Of course, skiing meant Whistler!

One day when we were sitting in the L'Aprés viewing the mountain and reminiscing about our recent trip, Kurt's heart attack and my mother's death, Kurt remarked that when his time came he wanted his ashes scattered around the mountain.

"Oh, listen to him!" cried Branko, a chap from Yugoslavia and one of the regular Sunday skiers.

"You're going to live to be a hundred!"

"I have a better idea," said Stan. "We'll meet up here in the year 2000!"

This winter there were still more changes at Whistler. There was a new restaurant, Rudi's Steakhouse. The owner was from Munich, and greeted us warmly, offering the best service we could wish for. Rudi's Steakhouse became to the Whistler skiers a friendly, cozy meeting place and we could watch him broiling the best steaks anywhere!

More and more people had come to Whistler, and many now had

their own cabins. I knew Kurt wanted to build at Whistler for some time, so when he told me he was going to put up some condominiums there I was not greatly surprised. I was surprised, though, in fact slightly horrified when he showed me where he was going to build – it was a swamp!

Our good friends, Ushi and Erhardt, came down to Vancouver from Prince George for a visit and so we drove to Whistler to show them our piece of land and tell our plans. We all sat on a log and with a bottle of wine christened our venture Edelweiss Village. That seemed a good name – after all, there already was an Alpine Village an Whistler Village.

There was not much to see from our log, and as it was too swampy to walk around, we decided to adjourn to Rudi's for refreshments. There we met Midge and Stan. When Kurt told Stan about his plan Stan immediately said, "I'll buy one."

"Don't you even want to wait until it's built?" asked Kurt.

"No," Stan replied. "I trust you."

We drove Ushi and Erhardt back to Vancouver, the narrow logging road reminding us of the narrow roads in Austria, especially where the skiing was best. But here logging was still going on, and one of the big logging trucks suddenly swinging around a curve toward one could be frightening.

Erhardt always carried a camera with him, and he spotted some bald eagles, so stopped for pictures. There are quite a number of bald eagles in these valleys; in fact British Columbia has one of the greatest populations of bald eagles in North America, second only to Alaska. According to the Fish and Wildlife Association, there are between five and seven thousand pairs in the province.

The Squamish highway wound past Britannia Beach, where Ushi and I had once taken the children swimming, and then on past the Britannia copper mine. This mine, which since its beginning around 1900 had produced enough copper to wrap a thin wire around the whole world three times.

When we arrived home, we were ready for a swim. Our friends stayed a few more days, and we did enjoy their visit. We reminisced about how we had first met years ago on the mountain, and in casual conversation had discovered we lived on the same street. In winter, when there was enough snow, we used to take the kids sleigh riding down a nearby hill. Ursula (Ushi's proper name) came to visit me many times, and it was the beginning of a wonderful friendship.

As soon as Ushi and Erhardt left, Kurt began work on the plans for our project on Whistler. He decided to build eight condominiums for sale. He had worked on bigger projects before this, but I'd never seen him more excited.

Kurt couldn't stop talking about his brainchild all through the Oktoberfest party (one of the first) given by our friend Leo at his home. Leo introduced us to a very good band, The Tyrolean Mountain Boys, to the Tyrol Club, and to two people who were to become very dear friends among the many we had in the Whistler community. The Tyrol Club, we were told, gave members the privilege of staying at Whistler overnight for a reasonable fee, and was managed by Trude and Helmut.

Helmut was a very cheerful young man, with light blonde hair; Trude was also blonde, and wore her hair tied back tightly in a knot. She was wearing an Austrian dirndl and we discovered both were fellow Austrians. Together we joined other dirndl-clad ladies and men wearing leather shorts in dancing, singing and of course drinking plenty of beer! As she and Helmut were leaving Trude invited Kurt and me to visit them in Whistler, and so we drove up one afternoon the to the Tyrol Club, which was located on the other side of the gondola station.

As we drove across the railway tracks we caught a glimpse of the beautiful Tyrol building, which was quickly lost again in the dense forest. We parked nearby and walked down the steep path toward the club. A separate, smaller residence we took to be Trude and Helmut's residence; there were flowers in all the windows boxes – red, pink trailing geraniums and a few begonias standing in wooden containers in front of the house. A wooden bench looked very inviting, and we could hear water running somewhere nearby. Following the sound, expecting to find a stream, we discovered an old-country water trough, and next to it Helmut chopping wood, a picture of health and Austria in his leather shorts. "*Greuss Gott!*" he greeted us.

The door to the house popped open and Trude, her golden hair down now and an apron in her hand, advised us "I was just making *Crammeln!* Would you like some?"

Crammeln! This old-world specialty is made from pork rind, cut in squares and fried until all the fat is rendered; the squares are then salted and eaten as snack food. Delicious!

Trude served us some more Austrian specialties, and as more people arrived, reached for her guitar to play for us all. "If anyone belong up here," I thought, "it's these two people: so much in love with nature and the mountains."

After the good food and good song, it was time for ski-talk, and everybody participated in that. Where is the best snow right now? What new equipment has been developed? Someone mentioned Banff as a ski resort worth visiting and Kurt was very interested. I knew we'd go there at least once! "But don't worry," Kurt offered. "When our house is finished, we'll only go to Whistler."

As I had expected, Easter of 1967 saw the whole family off to Banff. The local mountains had no snow, and the trip gave us a chance to see more of Canada. This was Canada's Centennial year, with celebrations everywhere.

Banff was crowded with tourists. Hippies roamed the streets carrying guitars and short skis. Short skis? A new fad!

We should have made reservations, as all the rooms were booked and we had to wait for a cancellation. We left our luggage in the hotel lobby and went sightseeing. As we were very hungry, we stopped for a meal first. The place mats on the tables featured highlights in and around Banff. There was Mount Norquay – twenty-three hundred metres of sheer ice, quite visible from our window.

When we returned to the hotel we found that due to a cancellation, we were lucky enough to get a room. The hotel clerk advised Kurt about the skiing nearby, and suggested we try Sunshine Village, which was very pleasant.

There is much more to Banff than just mountains: like emerald green lakes, thirteen beautiful hot springs, lovely shops. It is situated on the Alberta edge of the Rockies and the scenery is spectacular. Kurt Jr. took copious notes about all his discoveries, as he was studying about the Rockies at school.

All too soon, it seemed, our Easter interlude was over and we headed home with souvenirs and sunburns, looking forward to summer and our new endeavors.

•••

That summer we were busy building at Whistler, and it seemed so was everyone else, all getting ready for the ski season. All sorts of buildings were popping up – A frames, log cabins, even a tent village and some trailers. There was no centralized town planning whatever.

The Natives at the Mount Currie Reserve were very interested in all the activity. I'd never seen any of them on skis, but they came to watch the building progress at the skiers' haven. When we painted our window-shutters with the traditional alpine flowers, one of them suggested we paint eagles instead!

Stefan, too, came to see how our building was progressing and we asked him to build us some of his beautiful carved furniture; he was very busy, but promised to have it ready for us when we moved in.

When we drove up on weekends the roads were lined with hitchhik-ers, many from the U.S.A. "Skiing is better than the Vietnam war," they said, and we couldn't argue that. They worked a little and skied a lot, and Kurt envied them because he had to work a lot and ski so very little.

On hot days we would go swimming at Alta Lake, or at nearby Alpha or Nita Lakes. These latter two were not very big, but served the purpose of cooling us off. There was fishing there, but chances of catching any-thing was slight.

As well as the condominiums, we were building a duplex for ourselves, planning to sell one half. One of our neighbours from West Vancouver heard about it, came up one Sunday to look at it, and bought it – unfinished. That family had three children, and the parents thought the site would be ideal for them, being close to Vancouver. Midge and Stan, of course, had already pledged to buy one of the condominiums, so that left just seven units still to sell.

The condos were coming along nicely. Right next to them a doctor was building himself a castle! I was glad to have a doctor in the neighbourhood at long last; since Kurt's first heart attack, I was constantly worried that he'd have another.

The builders of the various projects were racing each other, and of course, the roof had to be on before winter. Helmut and Trude were no longer at Tyrol, but were building homes too, each more beautiful than the last and each with an individual character. Trude proved to be quite and artist, and did all the painting, and Helmut, a strong and fast worker, even had time occasionally to come and help us.

Meanwhile, in another part of Garibaldi Park a man named Adi was wandering around the hills searching for his perfect mountain. He was quite at home in this terrain, having grown up in Austria. He found his paradise at Brohm Ridge – a perfect location, not too far from Whistler and only seven miles north of Squamish. Alpine flowers bloomed in the profusion in summer, and in winter the snow was perfect. It was totally undeveloped, but Adi saw its potential as a perfect ski resort for V.I.P.'s – a Tyrolean-style chalet with guest houses – a whole village at the crest. He showed us an Austrian Christmas card that pictured his dream, which when completed would resemble that far away scene, and would feature the longest gondola-lift in the world.

He began the process of making that dream a reality. He had located a financial backer and signed Kurt to be the contractor, with work scheduled to begin as soon as the deal was completed.

The idea became a drawing, and Adi was so excited he wanted to begin work immediately, even though there was still far too much snow. He flew in material and men by helicopter and built a huge dome, under which they could work until the weather warmed up. When they erected the dome, the whole structure literally took off, the winds were so strong!

When the weather warmed, I went up to see for myself what progress had been made, and was amazed. Three alpine houses had already been built and the artist was putting the final touch on the giant chalet – a mural of a Tyrolean couple which covered the whole side of the chimney.

Kurt commuted between Whistler, Brohm Ridge and Vancouver. He was working very hard, and waxed enthusiastic about the development know as Brohmridge.

Adi flew many people up to show them his village, among them Canada's former winner of the Slalom gold medal at Grenoble. She and her husband were looking for a site for a potential ski resort, but after viewing the project and reviewing all the reports they decided to build at Whistler. Adi was unperturbed – he didn't expect everybody to like his paradise.

Our own Whistler condos were now ready for sale, and we advertised in the local Vancouver papers and also in Seattle, Washington, since many Americans were coming up to ski.

While Kurt was "showing" the condos, I stayed home to catch up on house and garden. One day Kurt came home earlier than usual and announced he had sold two units – one to a couple named Vivian and Roland, and the other to a judge from Seattle. I met Vivian shortly thereafter, while I was decorating the headboard of our bed at Whistler with coyote furs. We invited them for a drink and welcomed them to our little community. They wanted to know the mailing address, but lacking street names, house numbers and letter carriers, we suggested they use Edelweiss Village, which was the name we given the development. Our friend Stan, appearing on the scene at this point and overhearing that last remark, jokingly added that in Edelweiss Village, Kurt was our mayor!

Several weeks later two more couples from Seattle joined our village: Barbara and Jim, Marty and Karl. Jim and Karl both worked for the Boeing aircraft plant in Seattle. We sent over a bottle of wine to welcome them.

Even though summer had just started, everyone was busy settling in for winter, some bringing furniture up from Seattle. The Americans came up to celebrate their Fourth of July holiday, so we joined them in our celebration of Canada's Dominion Day (July First) and extended our festivities over a couple of days.

Although we usually took turns hosting "the gang" at dinner, one evening we decided to make a party of it at Rudi's. Rudi had the finest steaks anywhere, or would prepared something else to order if he was not too busy. Kurt always requested a dish called *Kaiserschmarrn*, and this evening was no exception. The name of the dish intrigued the other guests in our group, and when they asked what it was, Rudi translated it literally as Emperor's mix-up. That evening we all had Emperor's mix-up at Rudi's!

Winter came early that year, but we welcomed it. Our house was ready and we were anxious to do some skiing. Our children didn't come to Whistler with us very often now, as they had other interests – cheerleading and soccer – but everyone else was on the mountain by the time we arrived. We saw their lights shining in their windows. We had to shovel our way through the snow to our own front door before we could unpack our groceries and gear from the car. Stan came out to give us a hand and tell us the latest jokes, and Midge invited us over for a cup of coffee, which was truly welcomed.

As we sat around the fire Barbara and Jim came in and the conversation turned to equipment and ski fashions. Barbara worked in the ski shop, so was well-informed. Bell-bottom ski pants were still popular, but blue jeans were making a strong bid. There were new ski bindings on the market and fiberglass skis were still tops – with better techniques for skiing. Around midnight we all adjourned to our own homes.

We turned up the heat in our own cabin and were putting away the groceries when a knock on the door announced our neighbours Swend and Alvin. After our visit with them it was very late, but as we saw them out the door we realized it was snowing – Kurt was happy.

The morning brought more people: the doctor and his family; the

Seattle couples; our West Vancouver neighbours, Shirley and Bob. Shirley, like me, didn't ski much, so we usually got together for a walk or coffee and the latest gossip while the rest were up on the mountain. Our husbands were always the first ones up and the last down; sometimes after skiing they stopped at the L'Après for a drink, and brought home a half-dozen other people with them who didn't have a place to stay. How could we send anyone away, with such wonderful powder snow to share! And so we met Hubert. Hubert was one of our sometime-visitors. To watch him ski, one wouldn't think he was wearing a pacemaker. We welcomed all our houseguests! Now and then they brought us homemade wine or schnapps and all kinds of goodies from Austria. We talked about our homeland a lot – how it used to be – and about the war – and about the families we had left behind.

Driving home from Whistler on Sundays meant we left either very early or very late to avoid what was now a "rush hour;" but this particular Sunday was one of the long days: the highway was extremely icy and it took us six hours to get home, where the trip usually took an hour or less!

When we did get home we were very pleasantly surprised – Vivian and Kurt had dinner all ready for us. It was a little overcooked here and undercooked there, but it was delicious all the same. Vivian didn't enjoy cooking and we realized the effort she had put into this.

Then came our second surprise, which was announced after we had finished eating. They had had an accident with the car. What could we say? We were glad they were not hurt, and I was glad Kurt was not too angry.

•••

It was time to prepare for another Christmas – early shopping to do, the parcels for Europe to mail before October. I'd always enjoyed shopping and was glad now that finally I could send home some nice things. Living back in Austria was still a struggle, so we usually sent them some money as well, which they certainly welcomed. Finally the parcel was ready and, hoping everything fit, I mailed it and awaited the traditional parcel from Austria and its annual treat of Mozartkugel with anticipation.

This year there was no question where we would be Christmas and New Year's Day: Whistler, of course! I baked shortbread and cookies and packed everything I could think of, from turkey to toothpaste. Although there was a grocery store at Whistler, the stock was both limited and expensive.

Christmas Eve was still our special family evening, and now we had two Christmas trees to decorate – one for our West Vancouver house, one for the cabin.

Our plan was to leave for Whistler the afternoon of Christmas day, but we'd had a phone call warning of a forecast heavy snowfall, and suggesting an earlier start. Christmas morning, there was Kurt dressed in his ski outfit, toque and all, urging us to hurry. He took all the pleasure out of the gift-giving ceremony. I was very annoyed with him, and so were Vivian and Kurt Jr.

"What's the matter?" I asked him as he paced the floor, puffing away at the inevitable cigarette.

"It's getting late!"

"What do you mean, it's getting late – we just got up! (The man is sick – he has ski fever)!

When I opened my gift – a pearl necklace – I forgave him. Vivian got a new ski outfit which she wanted to try on at once, but after one look at her father she decided to postpone that pleasure until we got to Whistler. Kurt Jr. got new ski boots; he had outgrown his old ones, and these were more fashionable, made of bright red plastic and cut much higher. The mere weight of them frightened me. Kurt, of course, decided to open his gifts on the mountain – anything to hurry us on our way!

It was really snowing hard. Countless cars were stranded on the road, mostly driven by people who had neglected to install snow tires or chains on their vehicles. But even with snow tires, the going was difficult and we stopped and installed chains as well. We helped several cars out of the ditch as we snaked our way along, a few miles at a time. It looked as though everyone was going to Whistler. The cars kept coming, and the snow kept falling.

Ushi and Erhardt were to spend New Year's with us, and I wondered if they'd make it out of Prince George. I didn't know how much snow they'd had up there. Since Erhardt had injured his leg in the war and could no longer ski downhill, their enthusiasm was now cross-country skiing.

We finally arrived at Whistler, and saw that everyone else seemed to have managed the journey too. I could see a light in Stan and Midge's window, and there was her traditional Christmas bouquet of forsythia, the bell-shaped spring flower which she forced in her cabin each winter. Their dog came out to greet us – how can one little Schnauzer make so much noise? – with Stan following right behind. He helped us shovel our way into the cabin. Everyone was delighted – all this snow meant good skiing!

I was glad to get inside, as the wind was very strong and cold. Stan and Midge dropped in with a bunch of forsythia, and Vivian and Kurt went to visit friends next door. As we chatted about the weather and Christmas, our other friends dropped in, two by two. It seemed our house had become "Checkpoint" and eventually we became worried if anyone didn't show up. Our village had become like on big family!

Branko checked in, full of life and love for everyone, bringing some of his homemade wine (you can't buy better anywhere) and the latest weather report. We were in for a change and could expect a cold spell. Ruth and Leo, a couple we had met through Stan, arrived at the Tyrol Club. Kurt liked Leo, partly because we was such an excellent skier, and partly because he was our "music man" – always in touch with the latest hit records from Europe. In no time we were all dancing to his newest records. Everyone made a special contribution to the party. Roland usually brought his own home-made Danish pastries – sooooo good! There was plenty of food and drink for everyone and the records kept playing and the dancing continued until, exhausted, we called it a night. After all, skiing started early in the morning as everyone tried to avoid the long line-up at the lifts.

But that next morning was one we remembered for a long time! There was no skiing!! The lifts weren't operating because the winds were too strong – the temperature had dropped to minus twenty-five degrees Fahrenheit during the night, but with the wind it was more like minus thirty-five degrees Fahrenheit. Roland came over with leftover Danish pastries in the morning, and in the short walk from his condo to our place he froze his ears!

It was the bitterest cold spell we'd experienced since we came to Vancouver. People arriving at Whistler from Vancouver told us the pipes in their homes were frozen and someone quipped that the very ocean was frozen over!

At Whistler it just kept snowing. We had to go out for wood for the fireplaces, but otherwise we remained comfortably cabin-bound, eating, drinking and celebrating the Christmas holidays.

Trude and Helmut came for a visit. They had trouble starting their car, but perseverance paid off. We sat around the fire chatting and eventually ski talk took over – who was the best, the fastest. There was no doubt in my mind that Helmut was – he skied like a god, but funnily enough he was not hooked on the sport; he could take it or leave it, though Trude (also an excellent skier) would rather ski than eat. In the midst of this interesting argument we heard Swend and Alvin arrive at the adjoining duplex, and phoned them to join us.

Alvin told us there was trouble with the power lines at home, so we stocked up on candles just in case the problem reached Whistler, and brought in some more firewood. To keep the cars from freezing the men decided to go out every 30 minutes or so and run the engines for a while. This plan might have worked, but after a while and a few too many drinks they got mixed up in their timing and some fell asleep and forgot this task altogether.

By the next morning the electricity was off and we discovered we were running out of firewood and food. We began to worry – enough is enough, and there was enough snow here for three ski seasons. In spite of the conditions Ushi and Erhardt arrived from Prince George (much to our surprise) and we were very pleased to see them. It gave us an excuse to plan a New Year's Eve party! It was difficult getting around, as most of the cars wouldn't start, so we tried to organize a party close to home.

With no traffic in or out of Whistler any more – we were completely isolated – everyone share food, firewood and liquor – the latter very important as it kept us warm. And so our New Year's Eve party followed an old Scottish tradition – we went from house to house. In a very short time we had a veritable army of followers, all dressed warmly, not in the usual New Year's Eve finery.

When we stopped at Shirley and Bill's condo, we discovered they already had a crowd of their own. We wondered how they had all got there and were told they came by sleigh, but no one could remember where they had parked the horses! Shirley and Bill had laid on hot rum and all kinds of goodies.

There were many new faces in this crowd, and someone kept asking, "What do people do out here for entertainment? There's no nightclub, no big restaurant..."

"First of all," said the person next to him, handing him a drink, "we ski, of course. But if you're expecting to see Jackie O on the slopes you'd better go to Sun Valley or St. Moritz. Then in the evening we make our own fun, like now. *Prost!* Let's drink to that."

Later we wandered over to the doctor's house, which he had built with help from his family only. Of course, he had been expecting us and greeted us very warmly. He had a piano, which he played for us, and we enjoyed a sing-a-long. The singing continued out into street when we left. We didn't have to worry about waking anyone up, because no one was sleeping, not even the kids or the grandparents – besides, there were no police!! We sang in every language – Polish, German, Austrian, and Yugoslavian. After all those hot rums, spiced wines and Harvey Wallbangers, all strong,) it was time for coffee – and it was getting close to midnight. So we went to our place.

On the way to our cabin we realized we all had too much to drunk, for out of the night came a big sleigh with real horses – had Santa Claus been stranded too? Ah, yes, the crowd at Shirley and Bill's must have finally remembered where they had parked the horses, and treated us to the beautiful sight of a horse-drawn sleigh and holiday revellers!!

We reached our place just in time for the countdown to midnight. The cuckoo popped out of his little house and chirped that the New Year, 1970, had arrived!

Things returned to normal on Whistler New Year's Day – we had electricity again and a supply of food came in just as everyone, including the local grocery store, was running short. The cars were another story some did start, but others needed more that just gasoline. But great news for skiers: the lifts were running!! The skiing was excellent – New Year's Day is the best day for skiing. We had the whole mountain to ourselves.

Only one more day left, then we all had to go back to Vancouver. I knew this was one Christmas holiday we would remember for a long time! In fact, my thank-you letters to Europe contained a graphic description of our Christmas experience, including a picture of our snow-covered cabin at Whistler.

One evening the children and I were watching television, a ski competition. Kurt managed to tear himself away from the work he had brought home, he preferred working evenings so he could have the weekends free for skiing, and joined us. After a few minutes the children reminded him he was cheering for the wrong team – Kurt was cheering the Austrians instead of the Canadians! When Vivian interrupted the family's rapt attention for a moment to announce she was expecting a boy friend, Kurt's only question was "Does he ski?"

Kurt's 50th birthday was fast approaching and we decided to celebrate with a party. And what a party, and what gifts! The most unusual was a nightgown with matching nightcap, which Kurt immediately put on and wore all evening. Everyone was in great good humour, and Kurt was joking in fine form. Someone started to make a speech, and Kurt cut him of by saying: "Why don't you *postfone* it until you learn to speak English better?" Everyone roared with laughter, first because Kurt never could pronounce "postpone" properly, and second because his English generally was heavily-accented and not that good.

At midnight we cut the symbolic birthday cake, which had an uphill-downhill theme – skiers going up one side to a number fifty candle, then downhill on the other side! "Blow out the candles, but don't forget to make a wish!" prompted the whole gathering. He made his wish loud and clear:

"I want to ski until I die, then I want my ashes scattered on Whistler!"

"Let's have more music, Leo," Branko demanded. "Nobody is going to die: enough of this sentimental rubbish!"

When everyone left, I found Kurt asleep in his new nightgown – nightcap and all. "Happy birthday, darling," I said, but though he did smile in his sleep, I doubt if he heard me.

•••

Spring arrived early; it was perfect weather for skiing and with all that snow it should have been ideal, but Kurt was acting rather out of character – nervous and irritable. One morning when the family had gone I was reading the morning paper before starting my housework. I opened the paper and there it was – GARIBALDI GLACIER SHUT DOWN: BROHMRIDGE STOPPED WORK. Now I understood Kurt's depression: "My God, that's terrible!" I could hardly wait until Kurt came home for lunch.

"There's not enough money," he explained. "Now the investors are trying to get it somewhere else. The trouble is that so many people are against it – they all want to develop their own mountain in Garibaldi Park: Powder Mountain, Blackcomb, Whistler, Brohmridge – and instead of working together they're working against each other."

The developers and financiers were more interested in backing Canada's medal-winning skier in her enterprise than they were in listening to Adi, who won his medals for Austria. Those who had laughed at those crazy Norwegians, Austrians and Swiss who had tried the impossible at Whistler, tried to cash in on their new found success. The developers didn't care that those pioneers put their hearts and souls into those first undertakings. As Kurt had once said to me: "the mountains have my soul," and they had the souls of hundreds of others who loved the slopes and had contributed to their slow development.

Now the fickle backers had broken Kurt's heart and were instrumental in him losing all his money.

We did go to Whistler that weekend and stopped at Brohmridge as we always did, but no one was there.

Although there was perfect skiing at Whistler, sunshine and even corn snow, it didn't cheer us up. We came home earlier than usual and that evening, again we called the doctor and ambulance. Kurt had another heart attack!

Chapter Fourteen
Life Goes On

It was the same routine as last time. Intensive Care – that's the frightening part. Each morning I would phone the hospital to find out if Kurt was still alive; then all day would jump every time the phone rang, always praying -- until at last the patient was moved to his own private room. Miraculously, Kurt recovered once again and came home fairly soon with strict instructions to take it easy. That was most difficult for an active man, and when Kurt asked the doctor when he could resume skiing, he ordered him not to try it this season. Kurt smiled grimly.

Of course, he didn't follow the doctor's orders, and after a few weeks headed for the mountain. He felt it would be easier with short skis, so I got a pair too and insisted on going with him. Normally he doesn't ski with me, as I'm too slow, but this time he didn't mind. As we paused for a moment on the Olympic Run, who should cross our path but Kurt's doctor. He couldn't believe it, but Kurt assured him that he felt fine: he seemed to believe that his beloved mountains would heal him. In fact, as I write this, many years later, I note that doctors have recently determined that the danger to heart attack patients is in starting some new sport too soon, but to continue an accustomed activity is acceptable and even beneficial – and Kurt has skied all his life.

That evening there was the usual get-together with friends, but this time there was a newcomer – Art. Under questioning, he told us that he was a beginner, but he loved it. So right there in the living room we had an impromptu ski school for Art. Certain turns were "out" -- the French jump for one – and new ones were "in." Art soon realized that he was going to be closely watched by the gang, and criticized ruthlessly, but he didn't mind – he had determination and stamina. He and Kurt were both in the construction business so had a lot to talk about. Art knew about Brohmridge and though sympathetic, suggested we take out a mortgage and start again. Kurt listened carefully to Art's suggestion and mulled over the idea. Skiing was put aside for the moment as he said, "That's one way to start again, I suppose. Others have done it; I think I will too!" He felt somehow relived by this decision, and was more cheerful as he brought Art a glass of the wine which he kept for special occasions.

• • •

That summer we decided to visit the Prairies, a trip I really anticipated. That scenery would bring back old childhood memories for me! The drive from Vancouver was hot and dusty and we made many stops for cool drinks. At one of these stops we met Ushi and Erhardt, who were headed in the opposite direction, so we stopped and had lunch with them.

As we left the mountains for the Peace River country the scenery changed. The roadside was ablaze with wild roses and bluebells, bordering fields of wheat growing in rich black soil, or cornfields which looked like rivers of gold when the wind blew – so beautiful – so peaceful. The actual rivers and lakes of the area contribute to its unique beauty; I was not surprised to learn that this area has one of the largest river systems in the world. The rivers criss-crossed by rail lines, with their companion grain elevators standing silently silhouetted on the horizon. This flat country, so similar to the Ukraine, was the site of the filming of

Dr. Zhivago, and indeed Poles, Hungarians and Russians are in the majority here, Germans and Austrians having settled mostly in the mountainous areas. It was the same old familiar story: the immigrants searched for surroundings similar to the ones they left – the same sounds, smells and landscapes.

Driving into Grande Prairie, we drove to Edmonton. What a busy place was Canada's northernmost city, its "Gateway to the North." Everyone was dressed in period costumes for the city's Klondike Days festivities, so we were in for a special treat. The stores were displaying the most beautiful fur coats, and I just had to try one on: buying one, after the Brohmridge failure, was out of the question. Too bad!

Next on our itinerary was Elk Park, site of a little historic church built in 1861, where Indians and settlers prayed together. From there we went to Leduc, twenty miles south of Edmonton, where oil was first discovered in 1947, resulting in Alberta's becoming one of the major oil-producing areas in the world. When I remarked to Kurt that Alberta would be a nice place to live and suggested we move there, he just replied, "Let's go home." And that's what we did – headed for our home in the mountains.

Our first visitor when we got home was Trude from Whistler, looking very sad and disturbed. "I've just come from the hospital," she told us. "The doctors think Helmut has cancer!" After dinner we accompanied Trude to the hospital and found Helmut quite cheerful, full of news of Whistler and Brohmridge. Apparently there was a caretaker at Brohmridge, a Frenchman named Pierre, hired so that those lovely buildings wouldn't deteriorate.

As we drove home from the hospital there was little talk; everyone was busy with their own thoughts. We really loved that man and had become very good friends over the years.

The seasons pass no matter what transpires, and it was fall again. The leaves on the trees were now vivid orange and yellow and were falling all over the lawns. There were many things to do before winter – fruit trees to be tended, the swimming pool covered, the garden put into shape, and all before the weather turned rainy. Fall can be beautiful in Vancouver, and is usually warm.

Vivian began attending classes at the University of British Columbia that fall, which is situated in Vancouver on the tip of Point Grey and is surrounded by mountains and sea. The campus consists of some three hundred buildings in this beautiful setting, including the Museum of Anthropology which houses a major collection of Native Indian carvings and artifacts. Whenever we had visitors we took them there to tour the campus and visit the museum and the botanical gardens – then on to Robsonstrausse for European sausages and cheese and perhaps lunch in the Schnitzelhaus.

●●●

Kurt had to go to Prince George on a job and asked me to come along; he was planning to go hunting with Erhardt if he got finished in time, and I could have a visit with Ushi.

Hunting is very good near Prince George – lots of moose, which is good meat for winter. Moose goulash is very tasty and a nice change from beef. Of course, the hunter runs the risk of meeting up with a grizzly bear! And on this trip the men did come back with a huge moose; its size had posed some difficulty in carrying it out of the forest. But, once out, it provided plenty of meat for all of us, plus a trophy for the wall of our Vancouver house.

While Brohmridge was dead and Adi's dream buried for the time being at least, Whistler was very much alive. Kurt was sick about Brohmridge, but his motto was "the best medicine is to go to the mountains," even, as in this case, the mountains were the indirect cause of the illness in the first place.

We found Helmut up and around, a little thinner but in good spirits as always and still building houses, the newest just as prettily Tyrolean as the others.

There was a great deal of activity at Whistler now, not only skiers but developers. There was a marked difference in the structures built by those who genuinely loved the place and the ones put up by persons strictly interested in profit. In Helmut and Trude's case, the difference in quality really showed.

We busied ourselves cutting the grass that had grown in front of the cabin; we had planted the area as clover so we wouldn't have to mow it, but it came up grass. Had we planted grass, doubtless it would have come up clover. Some of our neighbours also had lawnmowers in action, while others were painting. In the evening Art arrived, with so many crabs we had to put them in the bathtub to clean them. We invited all the neighbours in for a crab feast.

• • •

In Vancouver we heard that Maria and Willy had gone back to Europe, for good. They told us they were planning to do it, but none of us believed them, thinking they were just homesick for Austria. Now the couple we had shared passage with on board that old, rusted refugee vessel had returned to the old country, on better transport than they had arrived at least.

• • •

My cousin Joe telephoned one day to ask Kurt to accompany him to Vancouver's annual Salmon Derby. The fishing started at sunrise and closed at a pre-arranged time, in this case, late morning. The first prize is usually a boat, and there were numerous other prizes for big fish caught. Joe and Kurt didn't land any of the prizes, but Kurt did land a new job that day, confirmation arriving in the mail a few days later.

The new job was in Williams Lake, BC, and as Kurt Jr. was going up for the summer months I went along to see him suitably settled in. I was pleased that he would be boarding at the new foreman's house, as they seemed a very nice family.

Kurt and I stayed a few days until the job was organized, and then went on to Prince George to visit our friends, Ushi and Erhardt. We found them at their cabin on Stuart Lake, where they customarily spent weekends. Stuart Lake is a beautiful spot, almost bush country; just a few Indian reservations nearby. The land where our friends' cabin was built was leased from the Native peoples, in fact, and as there were very few cabins we had practically the whole eighty-mile lakefront to ourselves.

The fishing was fabulous – just drop the line and haul out the catch.

Erhardt and Ushi were out fishing when we arrived, so we waited around until they came in. Lunch was fresh-caught fish, a real delicacy. The water was quite warm, so we all went swimming. In the evening we sat around an open fire where we were joined by some neighbours, the talk being fishing instead of skiing (as we were used to): who caught the biggest one today, who caught the most. The northern lights put on a fabulous show for us, and it was past midnight when we finally went to bed, to be lulled to sleep by water lapping against the rocks.

On the way home we stopped in Williams Lake to find Kurt Jr. settled in and happy on the job. This would be his first job for his father, who dreamed of the time when Kurt Jr. would take over the business. It was very late when the two of us arrived home in Vancouver.

It was a strangely quiet house. Not long before Kurt had started the Williams Lake project, Vivian had shocked us by announcing that she would like to move out. It wasn't that she didn't like it at home, she assured us, it was just time to get out on her own. She and several other girls were planning to move into a house not too far away, and would work in the summer and go on with their university educations in the fall. Arguing proved fruitless, and so she had gone with our blessing.

The next morning, after Kurt had left for work, I found myself wandering aimlessly around the house, unable to raise any enthusiasm for housework, unable to concentrate on any programs on the radio. I was suffering that age-old ache, the empty-nest syndrome. Both children were gone – their rooms were empty – the growing years were done. Enough of this! I went out to do some shopping, met a friend for a cup of coffee, and felt much better by the time Kurt came home for lunch. I even tried to cut the grass between rain showers in the afternoon.

• • •

That weekend we were off to Whistler again. The weather was ideal for a hike up the mountain, perhaps to pick some blueberries. Our American friends were up from Seattle, so Roland joined us on our hike. We drove to the Olympic Run and hiked up to the top, where we picnicked on sandwiches and beer. It was lovely and peaceful there at the summit, and we were singing as we descended. As we neared the garbage dump, which is not far from the Olympic Run, we quieted in anticipation of seeing bears, which would come to the dump to forage among the trash. We saw five of them there, busily eating; we didn't disturb them, and they didn't disturb us!

In the evening our friends asked us over and we soon had the season's first part going, with dancing until the early hours.

Chapter Fifteen

1974

The 1974 ski season was just beginning. There was not much snow on the mountain yet; everyone was waiting for that beautiful white stuff which makes children's heart pound louder and skier's hearts beat faster.

The government had announced plans to aid in developing Whistler, so we investigated the proposed site on our next excursion. We wandered into a gift shop where two Japanese tourists were trying to persuade the shopkeeper to sell them a display sign reading "Made by Stefan." Stefan had brought in some of his carvings, together with the carved wooden sign, and a phone call to him solved the merchant's problem; Stefan agreed to make another sign. The Japanese tourist proudly wore the sign around his neck as he walked around the village.

On our return to the cabin we discovered the Swend and Alvin had arrived. After joining them in partaking of one of Swend's specialty smorgasbords, Kurt and Swend began talking of expanding the duplex. One drink let to another, and by the time Alvin and I joined them, they were in a very expansive mood! The problem seemed to be whether to extend the sides, the back or the front of the structure. Alvin and I suggested they go underground, an idea which developed into a hilarious debate. Around five o'clock we decided the duplex needed a name, which should reflect Austrian for Kurt, Danish for Swend, Canadian for Alvin and Hungarian for me – it was not going to be easy! About seven o'clock we settled on La Bozenik – a little French, a little Russian, reflecting no one's heritage and everyone's humour.

Realizing that no one had thought of cooking supper, we phoned Rudi's and asked him to make us a cake with La Bozenik written on it. When he asked what the occasion was and what the name meant we assured him that we'd explain later, confident we could invent a meaning to go with our invented name. Of course, we'd all had too much to drink.

Even after partaking of Rudi's extraordinary steaks, we were still slightly befuddled, and when the cake was brought in, complete with candles, we were not too clear in our explanations. Actually, we found out some time later that Bozenik means good time in the Czechoslovak language, which we certainly didn't realize when we invented the word to describe our cabin!

The next morning we woke to a wonderland of snow; it must have been snowing all night. From our windows we could see the skiers coming – car after car. And then we saw a trailer we recognized: our friend Art, who was really a good skier now, had arrived with his portable cabin, which he plugged into our outlet as usual. We cautioned him to not take our house with him when we went to get his lift tickets, remembering the time he had driven off hurriedly without unplugging his trailer first!

The skiing was good that day: lots of snow and not too many people, but it was a bit foggy. We had a few runs and then Ruth and I decided to come down for lunch. As we walked into L'Aprés, we found Leo, Art and Kurt already there – they always came down much faster than we. Kurt ordered "delivered" eggs (he never did get onto devilled eggs) and the waitress cheekily asked where he'd like them delivered to.

During lunch we reminisced about the Alpine Musikband, which used to play the polkas, waltzes and other old-fashioned dances we enjoyed. Now there was a disco instead and the crowds were more Canadian.

Kurt's renewed hope in re-mortgaging Brohmridge and completing the project with government assistance had died – the government having opted to fund Whistler – and so the dream of three Austrians to build a Nordic Taj Mahal to their love for both countries faded into the mist of time.

•••

We had just received a letter from Austria inviting us to spend the next Christmas in the old country, and we were considering and discussing this idea when we had a surprise visit from Kurt's sister, Hella, from Delaware. After showing her around the Vancouver area, we whisked her off to Whistler.

The drive along the mountain highway was particularly spectacular that day, and the scenery was breathtaking. We stopped often so Hella could take pictures of the vistas; the sun gleaming on snow-capped peaks, boats of all sizes scattered across the surface of a deep-blue ocean and bald eagles soaring from trees so high they fairly touched the sky.

Hella loved our Alm House, said it looked Austrian, and quite understood why Kurt liked to come up there to renew his strength and peace of mind. She, too, was a mountain lover and missed the peaks more than anything else.

•••

Every year, when the ski season comes to an end, the Indians and skiers get together for a rodeo. We explained it all to Hella and she thought it would be fun to go. On our way she was still busy taking pictures, and we stopped quite often to accommodate a particular shot.

The Natives spared no effort in entertaining the skiers, and even had a Queen of Rodeo. There were wagon races, plenty of smoked salmon to eat, but you brought your own booze and shared it with the Natives. One Native decided to do a War Dance, paint, feathers and all. We all enjoyed ourselves, especially Hella.

92

Hella encouraged us in our half-formed intention to visit Austria at Christmas, and remembering our last sad trip to the Old Country, we decided to make the journey – no more putting it off until it was too late! Kurt's mother was still alive and waiting for us, and was so lonely now.

•••

That summer we went up to Williams Lake to check on Kurt's jobs and to see Ushi and Erhardt. Stuart Lake was lovely, the water nice and warm for swimming. Erhardt took us out in his boat, which he had made himself, and it was a very professional job, too. We caught enough fish to have some left over to smoke and take back with us.

On the way home we stopped at restored Barkerville, where there is a theatre which opens each summer and puts on productions for the tourists. Our daughter, our Vivian, was in one of the plays, so of course we had to go see it! (Vivian played her part very well, but I'm sure Kurt would have preferred her to be a downhill racer to an actress). The actors walked around the streets dressed in their costumes – Barkerville comes alive in summer. We had a good visit with Vivian, and later I collected some wild flowers which I put into a vase shaped like an old-fashioned shoe and gave it to her for her birthday. As I watched the passing scene, I wished Mama and Papa could have seen all this. I knew they would have loved it. But at first we didn't have the money, then we didn't have the time, and now it's too late. (Yes, we must go to Austria this year)!

The following weekend we went to Whistler again. Kurt always had a million reasons for going – the house needed painting; something needed fixing; and so on.

As we drew up to the cabin, I noticed something new had been added to our garden, and we saw that Helmut had been very busy during the week installing our own Austrian water-trough. There it was – just where we had planted the edelweiss and enzian. The water was not yet hooked up, but there was our trough surrounded by alpine flowers! I immediately set to work and planted some Indian paintbrush around it, and now it was complete – red, white and blue flowers! We sat and gazed at the scene raptly.

It wasn't long until Helmut came over and insisted on hooking up the water at once. We thanked him from our hearts, and tried to coax him to stop a bit and have a drink with us. He refused, reminding us that he didn't have much time left to enjoy helping his friends. This was a fact we had refused to accept, though he obviously had, and as he dug down into the graveled space, the water began to flow into the trough – at about the same time that tears began to flow down my cheeks.

Finally Helmut finished the task and sat and talked with us awhile about the changes taking place at Whistler. We all agreed that the original atmosphere of the place had been lost, but it was "progress," and it couldn't be stopped. Even in a big country like Canada, one can't have a whole mountain to oneself forever.

A few more friends dropped by and joined us in quiet talk, and thus we sat until late, watching the water dripping into the trough and the sun glowing on the mountains, the *Heilige Berge*.

Our American neighbours arrived during the night, and Roland's singing awakened us in the morning in time to partake of the delicious Swedish pancakes for which he had become famous. He didn't ski, but loved hiking. Vivian (his wife) picked blueberries for jam, and together they felt the long trip from Seattle was well worth it.

•••

This year instead of preparing a Christmas parcel for Europe, I prepared us! There was Christmas shopping to do for our children here (no longer children, as they had both moved out on their own) as well as for our family in Europe. As I shopped, my mother was much in my thoughts and the sense of loss was still very poignant.

Finally the day of departure arrived. Kurt Jr. and Vivian took us to the airport in the usual rain, but the weather reports from Europe forecast mainly cold weather and some snow.

The flight was very tiring, and the plane was loaded with people going home for Christmas. My thoughts were of other times and other Christmases, and as we crossed the Atlantic I remembered a little boat down there called the *Anna Salen* carrying us to Canada for the first time

– it was almost twenty-five years ago. Kurt slept most of the time – he had no trouble sleeping on planes or trains. Although he was still under doctor's care since his heart attack, he refused my suggestion that he walk around a bit to help his circulation, claiming he felt just fine.

I must have dozed, as I suddenly realized with a jolt that everyone was getting ready to alight. Europe! We're going home! Now we had two homes, and if I had to chose between them for the rest of my life it would not be an easy task!

We stayed in Amsterdam for a day and a night, so Kurt could rest and relax. We found our hotel with some time to spare before lunch, so using the hotel stationary, I wrote a letter home:

Dear Vivian and Kurt:

Arrived in Europe safely and on time, to the sights and sound of the Old Country – they are different – and I hadn't heard a church bell in a long time, and all those bicycle bells in Amsterdam! Everyone seems to own a bicycle here. You see more people – not so many cars – and that's nice. Dad is feeling okay and so am I. We hope you are all right too. Will write again.

Love,

Mum and Dad

The next day we left for Salzburg – not a long flight -- as the Alps came into view, Kurt felt wonderful. There were a few people missing from the familiar gang awaiting our arrival, but Kurt's mother was there and her happy shining face made the whole trip worthwhile. My brothers and their families were there, and I noticed for the first time that baby brother had grey hair. We were all getting older and it showed. But the important thing was, we were all together again, even if just for a short time.

We stayed at a hotel again, since nobody really had room for us in their small houses. Our hotel was close to both families and we visited back and forth, planning to spend Christmas Eve with Kurt's mother and the next day with my brothers, then a visit to Graz to see Kurt's brother.

Salzburg is lovely in winter, so we decided to walk everywhere. We could smell the sauerkraut and schnitzel from the little inns along the way, and listen to the familiar dialect as we walked behind people in green loden coats and Salzburg hats. Now and then we thought we recognized some person, but.... We stopped at our old favourite *kaffeehaus* – the coffee was a little stronger than we remembered but very good, and the cakes were just as delicious as ever.

We went to visit Kurt's mother, who was waiting for us. Waiting had been her pastime for some twenty-five years; everyone had gone, Kurt and his sister the farthest. She offered us coffee and cake, which we couldn't refuse, even though we had just come from the *kaffeehaus*. Her hands shook as she passed the cups and plates, but her face glowed with happiness.

After a long visit we left to visit Fritz, who had taken the day off especially to be with us.

Before we left, she did tell us there was one place she would like to go with us – the chapel where *Silent Night* had been played for the first time – and Kurt promised to take her there on Christmas Eve.

When we arrived at my brother Fritz's house, brother Max and family were also there. They wanted to know everything about Canada, the children asking the most questions. They were learning English in school and could speak it quite well. Fritz constantly spoke of Mama, whom he missed very much, and reminded us of things she had said or done. Finally the conversation turned to skiing, and Kurt told them that his brother had invited us up for the following week's opening of a new ski hill. We hadn't brought any ski equipment with us "Agnes wouldn't let me," Kurt told the group but we were sure we could get outfitted with borrowed gear .

We asked Kurt's mother to come with us to Graz, but she declined vociferously, declaring that Roland should be living in Salzburg instead of so far away!

Our rented car didn't make it to Graz, as there was a lot of snow, but we finally arrived at Roland's new home which he had just built, and were warmly greeted in a huge entrance hall. Roland proudly showed us around the rest of the house, a bit perturbed by Kurt's incessant smoking. He didn't smoke, and Kurt had assured him that the smell of the smoke would not linger on forever in his home.

Roland's wife had prepared a sumptuous dinner, to which she had invited some friends who also were anxious to meet the "Canadians." There was much talking about skiing in Canada, and Kurt, who usually championed Austria at home, now did a complete turnaround and praised Canada and its mountains, especially Whistler! During the discussion about the opening of the ski run on the weekend, at which the mayor would officiate, they told us that the skier who was to do the first honorary run couldn't make it because his father had died that afternoon. After much discussion, Kurt was elected to do the first run down.

On opening day everyone was already up on the mountain when we arrived. Kurt's brother was a little worried, but the skis and boots fit well, even though Kurt teased his brother about wearing such old-fashioned leather boots. Finally there was the signal and Kurt schussed down the mountain as though he was winning the Gold at the Olympics. His brother was very proud, pretending not to hear when someone in the crowd said Kurt skied better than Roland. We all went back to Roland's cabin, where he and his family spent most weekends. (It was about the same distance from his home as Whistler is from Vancouver.) Kurt promised Roland a new pair of ski boots as soon as they returned to Graz. We would have liked to stay longer, especially Kurt, but we had to get back to Salzburg for Christmas Eve.

Driving back to Salzburg was like driving through a Christmas card scene. Everything was white – cars carrying Christmas trees – people with parcels gaily wrapped, and then, right in the middle of the town the huge *Christkindsmarket* – booths loaded with every kind of gift: candy, chokolades and, of course, a *Wuerstlstand* with hot wieners for sale any time of the day or night. Christmas Eve, 1974 – a perfect time to visit the Silent Night Chapel with Kurt's mother.

It was a nice sunny drive out to Oberndorf to the chapel. We passed people carrying Christmas trees and children playing in the snow, their faces joyous with expectations, as ours had been when we were young. The Chapel sits between two huge Christmas trees, which were heavily laden with snow. People were walking around outside taking pictures when we arrived.

My thoughts went back to Canada and a cold wintery night at the chapel on Whistler Mountain. We were waiting for the priest from Vancouver to arrive to say midnight Mass, but bad weather prevented him from making the trip, and there was nobody who could perform the rites in his place. We didn't know just what to do, and as we sat waiting someone started singing *Silent Night;* then every one joined in and after the last chorus faded, we continued our impromptu worship with other Christmas carols.

After the services at the Silent Night Chapel, we all went to one of the inns, of which there are many near the church, as the custom here is to first go to church and then to the inns for beer or wine and a chat with the neighbors. In Salzburg, one doesn't just grab a hamburger and eat it on the run!

Now back to Grandma's house for Christmas Eve – my favorite time. The tree glowed warmly with real candles, and on the table were lovingly baked cookies and *pfefferkuchen,* which she served with hot wine. This medley of aromas evoked such strong memories in each of us that the ensuing silence was merely our with not to disturb the other's thoughts. Then the church bells started ringing, calling people to midnight Mass. For us it was time to open presents.

Mother liked what we brought from Canada – a carved bear and some clothing; for me there was a nice handbag and the traditional *Mozartkugel.* Then she handed Kurt an envelope, which he opened and passed over to me; in it was a cheque for $5,000. "But, Mama," protested Kurt, "I can't accept this – you keep it." But she insisted, saying that each of her three children got the same. She had saved it from her pension. What could we say? That is love, and that is what Christmas is all about.

Christmas day, we went to my brother's. Kurt's mother declined our invitation to come along, preferring to stay in the quiet of her own home.

My brother lived in an apartment and, of course, had a piano, which he played so well. His Christmas tree, decorated in gold and silver, glowed with real candles also. We all missed Mama and Papa; Mama, we remembered, used to make us a special Christmas cake from an old Hungarian recipe. Fritz's wife, Kaethe, tried to make it, but it just wasn't the same.

We exchanged gifts and I was pleased that the things we brought fitted, especially the blue jeans for the young people. As we were leaving, we made a date to go to the *Braustueberl* (Beer-garden) before returning to Canada. As we walked home the city was bright with lights, especially around church steeples, and the old 14th century Festung, the fortress landmark of Salzburg, looked as if it was made of gold. We were so glad we came!

Back in Canada again it didn't take long to realize where "home" really was. The kids met us at the airport and chattered all the way home about business, what they'd been doing and how much they enjoyed all the little notes I'd left them with their Christmas gifts. "Wait until you see what they sent you from Austria. It'll be like Christmas all over again!" I told them.

Ruth telephoned from Whistler the next morning to tell us about the plans they'd made for a New Year's party. They had rented the whole of Rudi's restaurant – no one had a house big enough. Kurt was very happy about it and couldn't wait to get up there skiing.

Rudi's was completely filled with our friends – other people had to be turned away. Rudi was sorry, but that's Snowbizz! As the evening wore on, some of the ladies were watching the door as well as the clock. Their husbands were working in Woodfibre, a pulp mill town just south of Squamish, and had promised to be there by midnight. Helmut had still not arrived, either. Only a few minutes to go! Then the anxiously watched door flew open and in they all came at once. "Happy New Year" rang out midst huffing and puffing. Happy New Year! 1975 was ushered in.

CHAPTER SIXTEEN

1975

Kurt's business, while thriving in the spring of 1975, had still not fully recovered from the Brohmridge setback, and Kurt was still hoping to compensate for it in some way. But the government chose to build upon what others had begun at Whistler, and Brohmridge was forgotten. Pierre, the Frenchman, guarded the unfinished dream, coming down to the village of Squamish occasionally for food and liquor, then back to his lonely life on the mountain he loved.

Springtime is my favourite skiing time – the weather is warm and the snow easy. Sometimes we hiked to the West Bowl and had a picnic, but the Westbowlers who claimed the territory as their own were not very hospitable. There were also Backbowlers and Toilet Bowlers, but the West Bowl was safest as there were no chairlifts or gondolas, and skiers had to hike up. The Toilet Bowl was usually busier since it was right in the middle of most ski runs. It was not a place for beginners, and because of its many lumps and bumps most skiers avoided it, preferring to take the Pony trail which ran parallel to the chairlift. The Back Bowl meant a ride up the gondola, then a transfer to one of the chairlifts and then a further trip on the T-Bar, which took the skier even higher; but then there was a wide-open space to ski down at the end of the journey! It was beautiful on a fine day, but the final trip on the T-Bar could be miserable on a cold, windy day. So, although it was about a half-hour hike to the West Bowl (depending on the condition of the hiker) it was still preferable. We would pack a lunch in a backpack, and pick a fine spot in which to picnic, our skis stuck in the snow, sitting on our ski jackets, leaning against the skies, the sun caressing us as we ate. Once, someone brought along a mouth organ and we sang along to familiar tunes; if we closed our eyes we could imagine ourselves in the Alps, or some other old favourite mountain, and we thanked God for this beautiful world.

One day we decided to ski the Green Chair, an easy run. Kurt had disappeared after a while for more challenging territory, and when I spotted Helmut I asked him to ski one run with me. He had lost a great deal of weight and seemed tired, but agreed and we skied down the Olympic run, planning to continue from the Green Chair all the way down to the village. But when we reached the Green Chair, Helmut decided to take it back up and transfer to the Gondola to ride down to the village. I had thought he was just bored with my skiing, but that was not the case; the cancer was taking its toll, and his stamina for skiing was ebbing, like his young life. He died that August, and the funeral at the Church was packed – some friends coming straight from work, others wearing the green Loden suits traditional of Helmut's hometown in Austria. We all remembered him, the healthy young man we had first met with the love for the mountains. His last wish was to have his ashes scattered on Whistler.

So it was done. His soul became, at last, one with the beloved mountain.

In September 1975, Whistler became a Resort municipality. Building was going on everywhere, and the municipality was hoping to host the next Winter Olympics, though they had been unsuccessful in their last bid.

We missed Helmut. He had always been somewhere in the village, and belonged to the setting as much as the trees and mountains did. Trude kept much to herself, concentrating on producing some beautiful art-work – painting on glass and wood. They do say that people in unhappy moments can create beautiful things.

When we arrived back in West Vancouver we had visitors waiting for us: Maria and Willie! I couldn't believe my eyes – they had moved back to Austria – for good. But no – once there they were homesick for Canada, and after much discussion and comparison, they decided they preferred their adopted country and so here they were!

We usually took our holidays in late summer, when Kurt could best get away from his business. Sometimes we would go to Whistler, some-times to Stuart Lake where we had a cabin a few doors away from Ushi and Erhardt. Since Kurt and Erhardt were both in the construction busi-ness they found much to talk about, while Ushi and I caught up on all the latest gossip.

This year our choice was Stuart Lake, with a stop at Prince George, where Ushi and Erhardt lived, for provisions.

The closest stores to Stuart Lake are in Fort St. James, a half-hour drive away and so we always arrived at the lake well provisioned.

We arrived in Prince George in the afternoon to find a tanned Ushi cutting the grass, and Erhardt still at the office. After coffee and some of Ushi's wonderful strawberry cake, her specialty, we began packing the car, as Erhardt had phoned to say he wanted to leave that day. We had just finished stowing the water, propane gas and foodstuffs when Erhardt pulled into the driveway and so, after a quick cup of coffee, we were on our way.

The drive to Stuart Lake is a beautiful one, through some dense for-ests, past a few Indian reservations, a sawmill, and the town of Fort St. James. Sometimes a deer flashed across the road, and we watched for bobcats, which would occasionally sun themselves on nearby rocks.

As soon as we arrived at the lake we went for a moonlight swim and then sat by the fire, watching the spectacular Northern Lights, listening to the loons and coyotes, and talking about fishing. Some neighbours drifted over and told us about their trip to Mexico, and as we talked about trips in general Kurt and I though it would be nice to go to Mexico for our twenty-fifth wedding anniversary, together with Ushi and Erhardt. We settled on February as a time of departure.

•••

Back in Vancouver, the days were shortening and Christmas was again drawing near. I started my Christmas shopping on Robsonstrasse – they had German Christmas cards there, which were especially nice for my mother-in-law, as she didn't read English. I met a few friends on similar errands and we had lunch at Schnitzelhaus. During lunch a man I had worked with back in Austria walked in, and we had a wonderful time sharing experiences. He too had first landed in Toronto, and missing the mountains, came on to Vancouver.

While window-shopping after lunch, I found a few gifts to buy, and then stocked up on sourdough bread and sausages, as well as a few buns and pretzels, which are all specialties of Robsonstrasse.

Going home over the Lion's Gate Bridge, I decided to drop into Park Royal shopping center and see the latest ski fashions at the Alpine Hut. Long jackets were on the way out – short jackets were new. Pants were higher, with overalls. I found a very nice blue outfit in Kurt's size and had it put away for Christmas. Kurt Jr. was talking about new ski boots and I looked at the new monstrous ones – they were getting higher and higher and were of course of plastic instead of leather. I just hoped short skis would stay in fashion, because I had no intention of changing.

Finally the preparations were behind us – now to pack the turkey, the tree and the gifts (which occupied just about half the house) and make for the mountain.

December 24 – and we were ready for Santa Claus. The tree was up, there was a fire burning in the hearth, and most importantly, the snow was falling. We heard Swend and Alvin next door, and across the way there's a light in Stan's place and blooming forsythia in the window. Soon Midge and Stan arrive with our annual bouquet of golden blooms ("What a lovely tradition this has become")!

On went the coffee and out came the cookies. Alvin and Swend arrived,

Alvin sporting a beautiful new gown which she jokingly called her new ski outfit.

Kurt and Swend had finished the extension to the duplex, giving us an upstairs and a mini-bar and much more room. We planned to plant flowers in the new window boxes which the men had made for us as an extra Christmas present; in the meantime, as our house is almost the first one you see when entering Whistler, we decided to decorate a big tree outside with lights: It looked very festive when finished.

Gradually the rest of our friends arrived, and we began comparing English, German and Polish Christmases. It always amazed us to find that Midge came from England – she spoke Polish fluently and skied like an Austrian.

Eventually everyone checked in – Leo, Ruth, Branko and Art wishing us a Merry Christmas, but they were only staying a minute since they wanted an early night, to be fit for skiing in this beautiful snow. But one glass of Gluehwein (spiced wine) led to another, and another; someone pushed the button on the tape recorder, and there it was, everyone's favourite tune, the unofficial anthem of our Whistler community – *Heilige Berge* (Holy Mountain). We passed the evening singing that, and other old-fashioned Christmas carols. The morning brought sunshine and powder snow, a Christmas present sent from heaven for all the skiers.

After breakfast our friends arrived to collect Kurt for skiing. Everyone sported a new outfit, a la cowboy – they all looked like Jesse James with a toque. Except Art. He wore the correct headgear, a very original blue-stripped cap. As Kurt tried to squeeze himself into his new ski outfit and I served coffee, Leo teased Kurt: "Pull your stomach in, Kurt. Mine is a little snug too; you just have to open the zipper after skiing to make room for some beer."

I walked over to the Gondola station with the skiers, not intending to ski but planning instead to photograph them coming down their first run. It was a short wait – it takes no time to come down. And there, you could hear them – yodeling, cutting patterns in the snow, happy like little boys – boys from the mountains of Austria, Poland, Yugoslavia. Knights of the Hills.

That afternoon some of Vivian's and Kurt Jr's friends arrived with skis and sleeping bags. There was Lori, Ken, Jim...I don't know how many but they were all heading our way. "It looks like they are planning to stay for New Year's!" I whispered to Kurt. He nodded his head, which I took to mean that it was okay with him. Most of our young guests had received skis for Christmas, and Kurt, looking over the equipment, noticed some ski poles too long, boots improperly fitted, bindings incorrectly adjusted. He pointed out these faults to the young skiers and they all took his advice very seriously. It was amazing how many Canadians were taking up skiing now: the new breed, the hotdoggers. It was a little easier for these newcomers – they didn't have to use all their energy hiking up the mountain like we did and Stefan still does. The skis are shorter, the runs longer and the ascent much faster.

We left the novices practicing in the living room as Kurt and I took Trude her Christmas present. Stefan was there and they showed us a cradle they were both working on for the first art exhibition on Whistler. It was hand-carved and painted with alpine flowers. I was tempted to buy it myself.

"What do you want to do with it?" Kurt asked.

"I don't know. Maybe put flowers in it."

"You're supposed to put babies in it," he remarked. "Agnes always has silly ideas," he told Trude and Stefan. Trude hastily changed the subject; she knew how Kurt and I could argue about silly things.

"Come and sit down over here. I've made coffee and there are Christmas cookies. Help yourself," she offered. I always liked to sit at her big heavy table with the names of people who had visited carved right into the wood top. It was, I thought, a nice, original idea. As we listened to *O Tannenbaum* on the record player Trude handed us our present. Actually this year there was one for Kurt and one for me. Kurt got a scroll, and as we examined it, she explained "There was this old wardrobe I inherited from Austria, which was shipped to Canada. In the wardrobe I found an old history book with the story of the Baumkirchner family. I did not know you where a nobleman!" she finished.

"Didn't you? Oh *ja!*" Kurt stretched himself proudly. "There are streets named Baumkirschmnerstrasse; one is in Wiener Neustadt. And did you not hear about the monument to one of my ancestors near Graz, which had its head chopped off?"

"No," Stefan said ironically. "Now I understand everything."

The scroll looked like an authentic antique, edges burned and all. Trude said she was afraid the whole thing would go up in flames when she did the edges. Kurt promised to take good care of it.

Stefan invited us to his house to see his Eistoeke (curling stones). We promised to come, "but you and Trude have to come out to our New Year's Day lunch. Don't forget!"

"*Was gibs?* What do you serve?" Stefan wanted to know.

"*Krenfleish* (beef cooked in horseradish). It is supposed to cure hangovers!"

•••

New Year's Day the word spread on the mountain about Kurt's remedy and in a short time our house was full. I was sure there were more people at our cabin than at Rudi's or The L'Aprés and not only skiers. June and Russ arrived from Vancouver; they were more and more interested in Whistler and its development. Kurt again told Russ to open a restaurant here, and the resulting conversation centered around restaurants in general with the resulting decision to give another party at Rudi's, this time a *Fashingsparty* (carnival).

"Kurt, your *Krenfleish* is so hot I need a fire extinguisher!" Bob was saying. Kurt handed him the bottle of Schnapps. "That will cause and atomic explosion! Give me some bread, someone, please!" Kurt was well satisfied. He had fun seeing tears running while people swallowed his hot lunch.

The conversation swung to skiing, a favourite subject with everyone. Something new! Helicopter skiing! The ultimate experience – skiing the Bugaboos, where a native Austrian has awakened the sleepy mountains in southeastern British Columbia. He was blazing the trails so we could ski virgin powder (every skiers dream). Everyone was so fired up over this news, and the Schnapps contributed to the volume so that finally it was impossible to hear oneself! I was glad when the crowd finally left and we had some peace and quiet! Once we were alone, I asked Kurt if this talk of skiing the Bugaboos would change our plans to go to Mexico.

"No, darling. Mexico is our twenty-fifth wedding anniversary trip; the Bugaboos can wait." The way he said it convinced me he rather have made a trip to the Bugaboos if only I was a better or more enthusiastic skier.

Christmas holidays drew to a close, and as we cleaned, packed and loaded the car, Kurt kept mumbling, "Some day I retire here. Some day I RETIRE ON MY WHISTLER!"

CHAPTER SEVENTEEN
OLE!

On our way to Mexico! Certainly everyone on our flight was having a
good time, especially one young man who was also on his first visit to that
country. He talked to everybody, smiled at everybody, and kept on down-
ing all those free drinks until we touched down in Mexico. As we were
escorted to the customs waiting room, he kept us entertained, but the
Mexican police were not amused; when he took their flag and started
marching around the room, it was too much for them. Two of them, their
dark mustaches steaming from heat and anger, informed our tour guide
in rapid-fire Spanish of what they were about to do. The rest of our group,
too scared to even talk, sat there and watched. A flag is holy in any country. They arrested the poor guy. The sentence was ridiculous – two years
in jail! He could, of course buy his way out for a huge sum of money, but
would never again be allowed on Mexican soil.

This unpromising beginning had us frightened and uneasy about our
trip. The hour-long drive from the airport to our hotel took us past bro-
ken-down shacks, though the barefoot people in front of them seemed
happy enough.

Our destination – a row of beautiful hotels, was another world. The sky had a violet colour, there were musicians playing in the garden, and the ladies' white dresses and men's white shirts had an unreal glow. White really is white here! It was not the detergent that did it, it was the sun. Our room overlooked the water; we could hear the waves.

"Let's go for a walk, now!" Ushi said. "It's okay, we'll just walk around the hotel area."

"It sure looks different from Stuart Lake," Erhardt said.

"No snow," Kurt remarked.

Erhardt went for his camera, even though it was getting dark. He was never without it.

"Maybe we should have something to eat first. Let's see if it is not too late." We went down to the dining room and as we were waiting for the waiter I saw a little mouse running about – and then another. I let out a scream!

"What is the matter?" asked the waiter.

"Look there!"

"Ah, it will not harm you, Senora. We have whole families here!"

I had not intended to eat after this, but then decided not to let a little mouse spoil my holiday. As none of us had any idea what to order, we settled upon a variety of dishes, some of which were good and some not so good. Most of it was spicy, and I liked that. Kurt liked nothing – except the beer.

Next day we joined the happy holidayers lying around near the water getting tanned – or burned – depending on their skin. There was Mr. Ringer from our flight. Ushi bravely signed up for a flight with a giant kite, and Erhardt busily photographed everything and everybody, including a Mexican who was fixing one of the straw sun umbrellas, chopping away with his machete very slowly. The splinters flew all over the bodies lying nearby as the man grinned toothlessly at them.

After a few days of lazing about Kurt became bored and demanded we do something else.

"But what?"

"Let's rent a car and drive out to the country."

"What a good idea!" So, the next day we rented a Jeep.

"The roof is not very good," the man at the agency warned.

"Who needs a roof in this heat, as long as the engine is good."

"Most people here don't have a roof on their houses," Erhardt was saying, "and yet they are happy."

We, too were happy with our green Jeep; "Remember the movie, *Four In A Jeep?*" I asked. "I think they also had a green one."

"It was a good idea, Kurt," Ushi complimented him. "Now we can see Mexican life and people; that's the way to see a country, not just see the tourists at the hotel."

We were all very excited about our intention, and without further ado climbed in the vehicle, which Kurt drove like a madman, giving Erhardt no chance to take pictures.

"SLOW DOWN!" I yelled. "We are not driving to Whistler, even though the road reminds you of the Squamish highway. And those truck drivers coming our way are much worse than the logging trucks back home!" Where were they rushing to? Normally people in Mexico took their time, but not the truck drivers.

Higher and higher we climbed, and I hoped that the car would not give out. It being almost lunchtime, we decided to stop at the next best place. Meanwhile, Mazatlan, spread out below us, looked tiny in the distance. Suddenly Kurt stopped the car in the middle of the steep hill.

"Engine trouble?" we wondered.

"Does anyone smell sauerkraut?" he demanded.

"Sauerkraut?" we all echoed. We assumed he had developed sunstroke. "Sauerkraut in the Mexican jungle? Is he mad?"

"No. I smelled it back there!" he insisted, and he turned the car around so sharply we almost fell down a cliff. Driving back a mile or two, we too smelled the sauerkraut and noticed a sign: "Villa Blanca." So we followed the smell and sign and sound of German marching music – *Schwarzbraun 1st Die Haelnus.* As we came closer, we heard someone singing *Lily Marlene.*

"The only explanation for this I have," I said "is that someone has tipped them off we were coming. Maybe the men at the car rental."

"Why? For business? Maybe when Hungarians come they have a goulash smell and gypsy music. Agnes, don't be silly. We will find out."

We never did. The owner made it quite clear it was none of our business why he was there. He was not exactly rude, but would not speak much to us even though he was German. The sauerkraut was excellent and we even had a Bavarian dessert. Kurt was so happy not to have to eat Mexican food he could have cared less why the man was there, or how he got there. So we left the mysterious place and drove on.

It got colder the higher we drove; the sun was setting so we tried to fix the roof but the wind was too strong – it kept falling down.

"If only we had a piece of string or something!"

"Let's ask at the gas station."

"How do you say 'string' in Mexican?"

"Did you not bring the dictionary?"

We found a gas station, but no string, so Kurt took off one shoelace and used it to fix the roof.

It was so cold we could have used fur coats. Who told me you needed just a little summer dress in Mexico? Obviously they had never been up here! "Let's go back!" everyone said. The beach below us looked so inviting, and so warm!

After a fruitful fishing trip and a couple of uncomplaining days on the beach our Mexican holiday was coming to an end. We had to start packing. On the advice of the jeweler, I decided to wear the beautiful silver bracelet Kurt had bought me as an anniversary gift. "Otherwise," the man warned, "they might take it away at the border. There is not another like it in the whole world!" he said, and I believed him.

Some of our traveling companions on the plane were almost unrecognizable with their deep tans, just like Ushi and Kurt. Neither Erhardt nor I tan well, but I was satisfied that I had tanned well enough for a redhead – just as long as it didn't peel.

At the airport, Vivian and Kurt Jr. were waiting with our coats, for in

BC it was still winter.

"There was some trouble in the business," Kurt Jr. was telling his father. "The foreman got sick and we were short of carpenters. I have been estimating and estimating," he went on, "but there are not too many new jobs and there is too much competition." Erhardt was listening carefully, since he was in the same business. "I landed one job, though, but not too big." It was enough – father was happy, and proud too.

The radio news advised that it was twenty-five below in Prince George, and we suggested to Ushi and Erhardt that they stay a little longer in Vancouver. But Erhardt said he had to go back to get a job to pay for the trip to Mexico. It was the first holiday they had had since coming to Canada, and although they had enjoyed it, "I am happy with Stuart Lake," Erhardt said.

"I keep saying to Agnes all the time, for me Whistler is a holiday," Kurt replied.

"For me too, if I didn't have to cook and clean."

"Don't you two start again," the children chorused.

That evening, we sat and talked about our trip, showing pictures and souvenirs and sharing memories of a landmark anniversary.

•••

It was time for the carnival at Whistler. Rudi had sold a lot of tickets for the festivity, but the weather did not co-operate. In fact, it was so bad many people stayed home. But Russ and June were brave; they came dressed in Roaring Twenties costumes under their fur coats. Midge and Stan were also present, and so was Rudi's wife, all three in Hawaiian garb. Kurt and I went as a cowboy and his cowgirl. Rudi made goulash and dumplings – no steaks tonight, he wanted to enjoy himself too! Still, even with the music playing we could hear the wind roar outside and some people practically got blown in; one of these wind-tossed guests wore a World War II gas mask!

We were dancing to the polkas when the phone rang; Rudi answered it, and came back to tell us there had been an avalanche. Where? We all wanted to know. They didn't know the exact location, Rudi told us, but someone had been reported missing and volunteers were wanted for the next day. This news had a sobering effect, and Rudi decided it would be a good time to serve coffee and pastry. Midge, sitting next to me, said she didn't feel all that well, and they planned to leave shortly. Kurt and I and Russ and June all decided we too would go back to our cabin; everyone was tired, anyway.

Back at the cabin I made mocha for all of us, and soon Kurt and Russ were back at it, talking about restaurants. "There is a certain risk involved, but look at Rudi!"

"Sure, it's easier to do it when everything is established!" Kurt encouraged him, lighting another cigarette. June and I joined in the conversation, building dream restaurants and in our fantasies, everyone's was better.

"I have the perfect idea," Kurt said. "A big place, old-fashioned on one side with old-fashioned dancing; a modern disco on the other side and in the middle...." At that point, he fell asleep and we were forced to wait until the following morning to find out what was supposed to be in the middle.

As I crawled under the comforter, I heard the coo-coo clock chiming and was too late to count the coo-coos to determine what time it was. I decided to wait until the next round, and fell asleep waiting. Suddenly, just as I got comfortable, the doorbell rang, and since it is no ordinary doorbell (an Austrian cowbell we had received for a Christmas present, its chiming can wake the whole neighbourhood!) I hurried to see who was ringing it. A glance at the clock showed it was 9 in the morning already!

And there at the door was Art, wanting to plug in his mobile home to our outlet.

"Come in, Art, and I'll make some coffee. You're still wearing your costume, or part of it. Where are all those feathers from?"

Kurt and our guests were getting up, so I made breakfast for all of us and we talked of our trips, ours to Mexico and Art's to the Bugaboos. "The weather was perfect, and so was the snow," he enthused. "The host was very nice. He's Austrian, you know."

"I know," Kurt said. "Some day I just have to go there." And there he would find another Austrian who had a vision in the snow and took the challenge.

Nobody wanted to challenge this mountain today; it was one of those days when on one went out who didn't absolutely have to. So we made a fire and sat around and talked of the past, present and future of Whistler, all the restaurants we were going to build, and how it all compared with other resort towns in Austria.

"Who cares about how many restaurants or nightclubs there are; as long as the skiing is good, I'm satisfied! The more things they have, the more people will come and I don't really want it more crowded," Art said.

"But you can't be so selfish," Russ answered. "To have the whole mountain to yourself – everybody should enjoy it! Don't you think God made it for all of us?" he demanded.

We all hoped that the weather would get better so there would be some skiing, as the following day we had to go home whatever the weather. We heard that the road was still closed, but was expected to open the following morning; and the next morning the Squamish Winds were still roaring as we drove home.

I wondered if they had found the people lost in the avalanche. Despite the bad weather, a search party had been formed but there was no news of the incident on the afternoon news. That evening, the report was that all those reported missing had been found safe, and that in fact the man everyone had been searching for had been at a friend's, having given up skiing and gone to a buddy's without bothering to advise his wife. He had heard of the avalanche and that someone was missing, but it had not occurred to him that the searches might be looking for him!

•••

The snow was melting, and another ski season was drawing to a close. Time again for the Mount Currie Rodeo. Every year, the crowd (ski crowd, that is) seems to get bigger. This year, we had a beautiful day for the event, and brought our camera along to photograph the mountains, the people, the waterfalls. We had sort of a picnic with the Indians with firewater and cigarette-smoke-signals. We have a little trouble understanding each other, but smiles can compensate for that. Not every Native speaks as good German as the one I met up at Stuart Lake. He was in the war, stationed in Heidelberg, and spoke excellent German. He told us all about his ten children, one of them blonde. As I poured into paper cups I recognized one of the Natives present as a man to whom we gave a push when his car broke down in Whistler once. I asked him if he remembered us but he just smiled.

"Don't you remember? We pushed you for a while, then someone else took over and so you got pushed all the way to Mount Currie. You were out of gas!"

We watched all the activities: chuck wagon races, crowning of the May Queen, the Indian war dances. Everyone was having a great time, and on the way back to Whistler everyone agreed it was more fun than the rodeo in Williams Lake, and still there was the masquerade part to come. People dressed up in costume and skied in it! Best costume wins a prize, and how one skis is not important. Kurt and I did not dress up, but we went to watch: Lord Nelson lost his eye patch, Napoleon had trouble keeping his hand in his jacket and skiing at the same time, and Mighty Mouse, Smokey the Bear and oh, look over there, Superman with a real kite, actually flying. "Isn't that Art?" Kurt asked. We could not find out – Superman had disappeared behind the trees.

Back at the cabin, I remembered to water the flowers in the window boxes. They make quite a show this year; people even stop on the street in admiration and take photographs. I had planted twenty-five trailing geraniums in each box to symbolize twenty-five years of marriage. The work had paid off and both Kurt and I were proud of the effect. Alvin next door had flowers all year round; she put artificial ones in as she said she would and actually, they looked quite good. It was just a little strange when they were still blooming in winter!

While I watered the geraniums, Kurt sat at the picnic table watching the water running into the trough. The edelweiss and enzian were also doing well this year, bordering the trough with blooms. Kurt was just getting up to go for a beer when he saw Stan coming. Knowing he prefers coffee, I went in and turned on the machine. "Would you like a cup of coffee?" I asked as he came nearer. "I just made it, and maybe a piece of cake?"

No reply. I thought he was ignoring me, and got angry.

"What is the matter with you? If you don't want coffee just say so!"

He looked at me sadly and said, "Midge has cancer."

Now I felt terrible. "You must be joking."

"No, the doctors confirmed it."

We all must have thought of Helmut at the same time, since everyone looked in the direction of the trough and watched the water catch and reflect a sunbeam. We just sat there, silently. Not knowing what else to do, Kurt went into the cabin and came back with a glass of cognac for Stan.

"Maybe there is a mistake; you could get another opinion from another doctor," I said.

"No mistake. We had a second opinion," Stan said, and poured down the cognac in a gulp, and followed it with another.

I finally did serve coffee. When Stan left, to pack up for the trip home, I saw he had left his pipe and when I ran after him to give it to him, saw tears on his cheek.

As we drove home, I notice how magnificent the mountains were in Garibaldi Park, and remembered how Midge loved this country, and ski-ing. I remembered her giving Kurt a shirt that said "Mr. Whistler," and someone saying "you should have one saying 'Mrs. Whistler,' Midge." I tried to think what to say when next I saw her. Does one talk about it, ignore it...what? In the meantime, we would pray for her and her family.

Midge made it easy for us all. She carried on with life, perhaps a little more intensely, skiing more often, enjoying the moments to the full. Stan and Midge were our guests for swimming at our Vancouver house one day, a visit that coincided with Doug and Laural's arrival from Calgary. As Doug and Laural had been our witnesses at our citizenship ceremony just twenty years ago exactly, we wondered if their visit had been planned as a sort of anniversary. We told Stan and Midge about how we met: At the time we were living in Cypress Park, and Doug and Laural were our neighbours. Kurt and Doug would mow the lawn at the same time, Doug with a power mower and Kurt with a push-mower. This went on for a while until one day Doug said over the fence, "Here, take my machine, it's easier." Afterwards they had a beer together, and a great friendship began.

"I call him Father Douglas," Kurt said, "ever since he became a Sunday School teacher. We had some good times together, didn't we, Doug? *Ja,* all those kinsmen parties! All those political parties!" As the conversation turned to politics I decided to *kaffeeklatsch* with the ladies; every woman likes a little gossip.

Doug and Laural left to visit other old friends and relatives, promising to drop in again before they returned to Calgary and as they were getting ready to go, Doug asked, "Are we going to Europe together?"

"We are, very soon," Kurt answered as he walked them to their car.

We asked Stan and Midge to stay a little longer, to enjoy the pool and stay for dinner. We planned to order Chinese food; I just loved phoning out for dinner! Kurt was not too fond of Chinese food, but he could always eat something else. Since the children left I found I did not cook that much. Before, I had practically cooked something different for everyone, as Kurt did not like Canadian food and the kids didn't like Austrian. It was kind of difficult at times, as I mentioned to Stan and Midge.

"Listen to her," Kurt mocked, "she has it so tough."

"*Ja,* it's true," I bristled.

"Now, now!" Stan calmed us down. "They know how to argue about the silliest things!"

It was a nice afternoon and evening, and after supper Midge and Stan had to leave to pick up their daughter. As we saw them on their way, I said to Kurt, "I really like those two." He could only agree.

•••

Doug and Laural dropped in again that weekend and Kurt suggested we show them our house at Whistler. The warm late summer drive was pleasant, since Kurt had no choice but to drive slower than normal so our guests could see everything.

"Everything has sure changed since I drove out here with my parents," Doug remarked. "It was only a gravel road then. Actually, only twenty-three years ago the transportation out here was by boat, and that was only to Squamish if I remember correctly."

"That's only a few years before we came to Canada. It must have been peaceful in Garibaldi Park at that time, only a few people on the mountains, and they would mainly be Indians, who would not be there to ski," I said.

There were some mountain climbers practicing on The Chief, and in the background we saw Diamond Head sharp against the sky. We drove up past the other peaks: Black Tusk, Powder Mountain; then Whistler came into sight and as we arrived I was happy to see all the flowers in full bloom. We had not had rain for some weeks and I had been afraid they would all be dead, but Trude had watered them faithfully in our absence.

Doug and Laural seemed to like our Whistler retreat, and after lunch we drove them around Alta Lake. There were a number of new buildings, and Doug remarked on one that resembled Frankenstein's Castle, as he called it. Architecturally, the area is very interesting as there is a mixture of styles. Laural pointed out one that she called a Barbarian Chalet.

"It's Bavarian," I gently corrected her.

The alpine styles that predominate, I explained, make more sense in this climate. The windows are smaller, so the cold stays out, and the roof is not flat so the snow can't sit on it and crush it with accumulated weight.

"Everybody has a different idea of a dream house, and the Austrians just build better in this area because they are used to this type of territory," Kurt said, "just like skiing for instance. It was Austrians, Swiss and Norwegians who showed people here you can do other things on a mountain than just look at them."

"Oh, yeah," Doug joked. "You show them how it's done!"

We decided to go for a beer and at the same time visit Russ and June.

"You know them," we told Doug and Laural. "You went to school together! They are managing the Highland Lodge now."

"I didn't know they liked mountains!" they exclaimed.

"They do now," said Kurt, lighting another cigarette. "A lot of people developed a sudden love for them. Even politicians like to talk about 'the family heading for the hills each week.' This seems to be the in thing right now, so they think to join the 'in-crowd' and gain votes that way."

We arrived at Highland Lodge and discovered that Russ and June were in Vancouver, as their daughter, Lori, informed us. We ordered our beer anyway and joined a few other acquaintances in the bar, where we talked about Whistler. An American at the next table overheard our conversation and joined in by saying, "People here should have a look at Alpenthal; that's the perfect ski resort, very authentic."

"It depends on what you call authentic," we replied. "Not everyone wants Swiss sex appeal in a ski development. Maybe our Whistler should be more Pacific West Coast."

"You could argue that," the American shot back, and so we did, until it became too warm in the bar and we decided to pay a visit to Trude.

Trude was also not home, but we looked at the house from the outside and Kurt said, "Now this is a house built with tradition, skill and a lot of love." As he wandered about, pointing out this detail and that, he reminded himself "I have to pick up some lumber to fix the patio. It collapsed from the heavy snow last winter."

"Is there a place you can get lumber out here?" Doug wondered.

"Yes, there is now. Before, we had to haul everything from Vancouver or Squamish."

By the time we had picked up our lumber, it was so hot we decided to go for a swim at Alta Lake, which being fairly small and quite shallow, keeps the water pleasantly warm for an Alpine lake. A few sailboats were out, and someone was attempting to water-ski; the noise from the outboard engine was very disturbing to the idyllic scene, and I hoped the proposed ban on powerboats on the lake would soon be in place!

Back at the cabin, we noticed we had had an intruder – flowers were ripped out, the garden furniture knocked over, and the "juvenile delin-quent" responsible was making good on his escape – a little black bear cub, looking for his mother, no doubt. Before Laural could get her camera ready, he had disappeared.

Our good neighbour, the doctor, and his wife were both out painting their new castle and as soon as the wife saw us, she came over to tell us how her mother-in-law, who had been visiting from Scotland, had enjoyed the flowers in our window box. The flowers did look nice, especially set underneath the shutters painted in alpine motif. Perhaps next year we should paint them in the blue of the enzian, I thought. Everything was beginning to look a bit faded in contrast to the bright flowers. I remem-bered a Native had once told us it would have looked better had we painted Indian paintbrush and eagles on our shutters.

That evening we sat outside, watching the cars pass and the stars come out (these made a spectacular showing that night). In the morning, we drove Doug and Laural out to the airport and promised again to make that trip to Europe together. We had been talking about that journey for twenty-five years now, and we began to feel we couldn't afford to wait much longer – we would be too old if we waited another twenty-five years!

Chapter Eighteen

Another Silver Anniversary

October 19, 1976 – exactly twenty-five years ago to the day and hour and minute. This was the day a lot of people had arrived in Canada, including Maria and Willie, and we were all going out to celebrate. The Bayshore was our choice – nice, new and right on the waterfront so we could watch the boats, though I was sure we would not see the *Anna Salen* here. I had read that the old ship had burned down some time ago.

I noticed quite a mix of people as I sat and looked around. A Japanese family was over there, a Chinese couple in the corner, French and Italians talking with their hands: I thought, what would Canada be if all of us had stayed home? Japan would be the only place we could get saki, and only in China could you order chow mein.

"Agnes, what is the matter with you?" Maria said. "Are you dreaming again? Let's order one of those drinks that the waiter is carrying over to that table," she suggested, "the one in the coconut, with a gardenia in it!"

I noticed that customers took the coconut and gardenia away with them as souvenirs, and agreed to order the drinks. It was pretty strong stuff, and under its influence our voices got louder. We ordered all sorts of drinks – Hawaiian, Polynesian, and in between them, German wine, Austrian beer – and so eventually the whole room heard what we were celebrating and began buying us drinks. As one of the men from the neighbouring table was leaving he said, "if you try all the drinks which were bought to Canada from somewhere else, you will be here a long time."

We had so many things to remember – "Remember, Maria, the girls on the boat and what you would say to them when they came in late? One time you waited for them and really bawled them out. They used to wake you, especially the one girl who slept in the bunk above you. You said, 'Aren't you ashamed of yourself, running around all night long with sailors?' And she calmly replied, 'What do you take me for – SAILORS?' I only go to the CAPTAIN.'"

Yes, Maria remembered, and laughed at the memory with us. We all remembered the storm in which Kurt and Willie had to be strapped to their beds. They were at the very end of the boat.

We remembered the policeman and the little flower he had carried all the way from Graz to his aunt in Canada. We wondered where he, and our other fellow passengers were now.

Finally we left, late, with our coconuts, our gardenias, and our refreshed memories.

At home, Kurt and I went to bed but I could not sleep, still wandering around memory lane. I recalled the time we made the decision to go to Canada, the sorrow of our parents when we left; without money or security, we must have been crazy. But often the young are just that, and being young and in love all we had were dreams and fantasies.

Not all our fellow émigrés succeeded in Canada. I recalled one couple who would have been better off not to come; they always wanted to go back to Austria, but never had the money. Perhaps they would have made a success in Austria; perhaps we would have, too, but it would have taken longer. Not everybody reached their goals here and some did even better than they had hoped. It had been, after all, our free choice to come. What if....

My thoughts were interrupted by the telephone ringing. I looked at the bedside clock – it was well past midnight. Who could it be? It must be Europe calling! They always call at this time, it seems. I had a queer feeling and answered the phone with some foreboding.

"Europe calling," said my brother, Fritz.

"My God, what now," I thought. I was so relieved when he said he was coming to Canada that I hung up quickly and immediately woke up Kurt to tell him Fritz was coming for a visit.

"When?" Kurt asked.

"I forgot to ask in the excitement, but I am sure he will send a telegram. I will be ready even if he comes tomorrow!"

After that it was even more difficult to sleep, yet I must have drifted off for I spent the night in Austria, and my brothers and parents were all there – but was it a dream or a daydream?

Suddenly it was time to make breakfast; Kurt was already in the shower and would soon have to leave for the office. He usually had only a few cups of black coffee and cigarettes. The doctor warned him to eat a proper breakfast and I try to make him eat the eggs and bacon or cereal that I have prepared – but I usually end up eating them myself.

It was a bit chilly in the house and I turned up the thermostat. It was raining again – I thought that people don't tan in Vancouver, they just rust.

The mailman brought Fritz' telegram, which said he would be arriving the following weekend to spend a little time with us before going on to a hotel convention in New York.

I began preparations: polished the house, tidied the garden, called in a piano tuner (Fritz loves to play and the piano needed tuning anyway).

I phoned all my friends for suggestions for meals, and most of them told me to cook European, except for one, who told me that since Austrians eat Schnitzel and Pork all the time, I should cook a turkey. I took her advice.

Vivian and Kurt Jr. came with us to the airport to pick up Fritz, and asked us how we would recognize Uncle Fritz.

"He is very tall, and nobody ever had trouble recognizing DeGaulle," I replied. I was interrupted by the announcement that the plane had landed, and there, among the passengers, was a tall man, the only one wearing a hat – our Fritz!

After the usual kissing and hugging we offered to collect his luggage, but, "oh, the luggage – it went in the wrong direction," Fritz mumbled. Well, we could look after that later – we'd call from home and trace it.

As we drove home, usually an hour's journey, Fritz, looking out the window said, "Really you don't have to take me on a sightseeing tour right now!"

"What tour? We're just going home!"

"Don't you live in Vancouver?"

"Yes, but in West Vancouver, which is a long way from the airport. Vancouver is a little bigger than Salzburg," we reminded him.

At home, I finished the dinner preparations while Fritz wandered around the house with Kurt. "Well done, Kurt. Congratulations," I overheard Fritz say. "I am impressed. Maybe I should come to Canada!"

"Dinner is served!" I announced. But as soon as Fritz saw the turkey, he said he was not really hungry. As it turned out, he could not eat poultry, which was my mistake. We offered him something else, but what he really wanted, he said, was a beer. Kurt brought him a bottle of Steffl beer, an Austrian brand that Fritz was not expecting to see here.

"Oh, we have everything in Canada now. You will be surprised."

We talked until we were exhausted, and next morning before breakfast Kurt and Fritz were out for a swim. Later, after Kurt had left for work, Fritz told me, "I wish Mama and Papa could have seen all this – they worried about you so much."

I took Fritz to Robsonstrasse to window shop, and once again Fritz was amazed at the varieties of pretzels and sausages in the delicatessens. "You can buy anything here," I told him. "I always get my Hungarian paprika here, for goulash." And reminded of this spice, I immediately bought some.

For lunch, we went to the Schnitzelhaus and celebrated with beer with our meal – quite different from Kurt's and my first Canadian restaurant meal.

A trip to Stuart Lake would be an experience for Fritz, we thought, and so we packed up the car, let Ushi and Erhardt know we were coming, and tried to make Prince George in one day. We would spend the night in Prince George, then move on to Stuart Lake the following day.

Fritz loved the trip, and kept saying that the country had so many similarities to Austria – it was just ten times bigger!

The following day, we stopped at Fort St. James for something to eat; Fritz suddenly pulled my arm and pointed at some people nearby. "Are those real Indians over there?" he asked.

"Yes, they live nearby. There are two Indian reservations within walking distance of our cabin, and we are actually leasing the land from them," we told him. He could hardly wait to get there – Indians were only something he had read of in Rolf Doring books.

The lake was calm and quiet, and as we looked across the water we saw an Indian paddling his canoe, bare-chested and gleaming in the sunshine. "I wouldn't mind living here, myself," Fritz declared. But we told him that it gets quite cold in winter, and one is cut off from everything. Even the Indians used to move to warmer climates in winter, when they were free to live their nomadic way of life. Now, of course, they no longer do that.

"Erhardt and Ushi came here once in winter, with their cross-country skis, and had a real tough time getting to the cabin," I told Fritz. "But Erhardt comes here in the fall for hunting often.

"What do they hunt for?" he wanted to know.

"Moose, bears, even grizzly bears."

"Are there any now?"

"Sure," Kurt answered. "Erhardt told me they saw one *Gesterday*."

"*Gesterday?*"

"Kurt always says 'Gesterday' for 'yesterday,' since '*Gestern*' in German means yesterday, he combined the two words and invented his own word," I explained.

Kurt readied the boat and asked Fritz to go fishing with him for a while. I was sure my little brother had never fished like that – they caught a few trout, which we had for supper, and later we walked over to the Indian village. Fritz hesitated a little at this suggestion, but it so happened that there was a Native coming our way who was greeting us in German and Fritz almost lost his voice – in astonishment.

Back at the cabin, we built a fire in our wood stove, and it got very cozy. We had no electricity at the lake, which was how most people liked it. We could get water from the lake, but for cooking we brought water in from Fort St. James or Prince George.

On the way back, Fritz kept declaring that he had to come back some day; it was so beautiful! We stopped again at Prince George for *kaffee* and *kuchen* with Ushi and Erhardt, then on to Barkerville to show Fritz the ghost town. Most of the attraction was still closed, but even so we had a box full of film to drop off at the pharmacy to have developed before Fritz was due to leave.

Vivian and Kurt Jr. surprised us with dinner, and I was glad I wouldn't have to start right in cooking. But Fritz looked at the hamburgers and said he wasn't hungry, and as Kurt was not too fond on them either I put a plate of cold cuts on the table for them. Kurt Jr. and Vivian were disappointed, but I reminded them of our trip to Europe and how they had hated grandmother's cooking, wanting peanut butter sandwiches instead. So we all laughed, and the situation was resolved.

That evening I asked Fritz to play us something on the piano, and after a few traditional selections Kurt Jr. asked "Don't you play rock and roll?" So he switched from Beethoven to Beatles, and we bridged the generation gap. "Tomorrow, we'll take you to the 'Crazy Horse,'" Vivian said. "It's a night club."

"That would be fine; I like night clubs," Fritz assured her.

Finally, we drove up to Whistler. I was glad it wasn't raining, and we could see all the mountains in Garibaldi Park.

"What a beautiful highway!" Fritz exclaimed. "It's almost as nice as the one in Trieste!"

We stopped at Brohmridge just outside Squamish and noticed all kind of equipment on the bottom station which Kurt had built. When we asked, we were told that they were taking things down from the mountaintop and hauling them to Whistler. We discovered that Pierre, the French watchman, had died. All this whetted Fritz' curiosity and so as we drove on to Whistler we told him the story of the Austrian's search for the perfect mountain, the dream of the ski resort at Brohmridge, and its near-success thwarted by the government's developers' preference for other mountains.

Kurt's voice changed as he bitterly described the collapsed dream.

"Why are you so upset, Kurt?" Fritz asked. "You always told me you loved Whistler."

"Oh, *ja*, I do, but there are two hundred and fifty thousand dollars of mine up there – " he pointed toward Brohmridge). Two hundred and fifty thousand dollars! I was the contractor who built the things they are taking down now."

"How did you manage?"

"We mortgaged the house and started all over again."

"I guess you can lose it as quickly as you make it in this country; but you can do that anywhere, in Austria too."

"Let's talk about something else, or Kurt will get another heart attack," I said. "He got his first one from all this. Now, look over there, isn't that just beautiful, all those golden leaves? Fall is painting his colours. I would like to pick some for myself and Midge – she loves them. I have invited her and a few friends to meet you. She has cancer," I told Fritz. "She's a very good friend of ours, and our neighbour on Whistler. A lovely person. She always brings me forsythia on Christmas day, and I bring her leaves in the fall. It's our tradition."

Even though it was late summer, the flowers were still blooming in the window boxes. "I left them so you could see them, Fritz, but I guess I'll have to take them in now, before the frost."

"That's your house?"

"Actually, only half of it; we sold the other half of the duplex."

"It's just like the Alps here," Fritz commented.

"Kurt will drive you around so you can see the rest of the place while I get ready for tonight."

Midge saw us arrive and came out to greet us. I handed her the bunch of leaves, and noticed how much thinner her arms had become. She had lost a lot of weight, and her hair was thinner too, but her spirit was as strong as ever.

"So this is your little brother," she said, looking up at the tall man. We chatted with her outside the house for a while, and Midge teased Kurt that Fritz spoke better English than he did!

"Where did you learn to speak English so well?" I asked Fritz as we went in the house.

"Well, dear sister, you have been gone twenty-five years, and a lot of things have happened you don't know about."

He was right; I had been gone a long time.

Kurt served some beer and wine, and I put out cold cuts; it seemed Fritz liked that better than anything. As we were unpacking Trude popped in to say hello. She brought me some flowers and said she would be back later. Fritz was amazed that everyone spoke German.

"It's like being in Austria!"

Leo arrived with the latest hits from Europe and we were listening to them when Branko and his wife arrived with their visitor, a lady who spoke neither English nor German. We wondered how we would start a conversation with her when Fritz surprised us again, and began a dialogue with her in fluent French! "It's my business to speak many languages," he said, as if he could read my thoughts.

"I must have been gone a lifetime," I thought. "I don't know my own brother any more."

"If you work in any hotel in Europe," Fritz explained, "you have to speak more than one language. Do you know Pierre Trudeau stayed at our hotel once? He gave me a pen and pencil set," which he then displayed for us. "As a matter of fact," he continued," Trudeau slept in the same room Hitler once did."

"Did he know that?"

"I'm not sure," Fritz replied.

Fritz' business gave him a wealth of stories, and I asked him to tell again the one about the poodle, the carpet and the Austrian Chancellor.

"Well," he began, "We have a number of old Baronesses and Countesses who have lived at the hotel for some time; one of them has a French poodle which she takes for walks once in a while. One morning she was doing just that while the hotel staff was preparing for the reception of the Austrian Chancellor and his entourage. We had just rolled out the red carpet when the Countess came back with her poodle. He must have forgotten what he had gone outside to do, because he did it right there, in the middle of the red carpet. I was trying to clean it up, but the Countess decided to engage me in conversation!

Finally the bellhop came running in: the chancellor was on his way! There was no time to clean up the mess, so I took a chair and put it over the spot. But the hotel Director came and wondered what a chair was doing there in the middle of the carpet and had it removed. At that point, in walked the Austrian delegation, and we all watched in horror as by some miracle each person stepped past, or over the mess without breaking stride.

Everyone was roaring with laughter at this when Art and Trude arrived. Of course they wanted to know what was so funny, and we explained that we had been telling anecdotes. She promised to tell one as soon as she caught her breath, for she had ridden over on her bicycle.

Trude is always exercising, to keep fit for skiing and teaching skiing.

Before she could start her story, Fritz, who had been conversing with the French lady, produced another volley of laughter. Immediately we demanded to have the joke translated into English or German, and he obliged. "I was just telling her of the time the French tourist came and asked where he could park his car. I got the words mixed up and told him to put it in the river. I meant to say, beside the river; anyway, I didn't catch my mistake right away, and the tourist kept saying it was not possible to park where I had said."

"That's almost what happened to me," Trude said. "A lady came for her ski lesson at the top of Whistler. She was there in time, but without her skis. 'That's impossible,' I said. We carried on like this for a while, and finally went back down to the village." Trude was full of news about the new mountain being developed, which had been named Blackcomb. She believed there would be good skiing there when it opened in 1980 as planned. There were also new lifts planned for Whistler; the village would be relocated to that side of the mountain where the garbage dump was now. "Too bad Brohmridge didn't go ahead; Helmut had thought it would be a good ski area," Trude said.

"Maybe it still will be, someday when we are dead," Kurt replied bitterly.

"Now, who's talking about dying?" Branko asked. "Let's have some music; where's Leo, our *Musikmeister?*"

Because the weather was warm and the air in the cabin smoky, we had the door open and people just kept coming through it – our American friends from Seattle completed the crowd, our big, happy, Whistler family. Soon we sang a new version of the old song; "These are the days, my friends, we wish they'd never end."

•••

The next day we drove to the Mount Currie Indian Reserve. "Interesting," Fritz noted, "how the reserve begins where the pavement ends." We had noted the same thing at Fort St. James. The Indians were sitting outside their homes, watching us watching them. Eventually we became uncomfortable at this, and decided to turn around and go home to Whistler. After a stop at Green Lake, we visited Leo and Ruth and their cabin, which is next to the golf course. Leo offered Schnapps and Ruth prepared coffee and Blackforest cake and we stayed a while, listening to music and watching the golfers and would-be golfers.

The next day we left Whistler and drove Fritz to the airport for his flight to New York. We promised to make the trip to Austria soon, perhaps the next year, in company with Doug and Laural.

"And on that trip," I promised, "I will visit Wiener Neustadt. Remember, Fritz, that long march so long ago?"

"I remember, sis. It's time you went there," Fritz replied. "I was there two years ago. It hasn't changed all that much. You must be sure to take Kurt to Baumkirchnerstrasse!"

And then again there were goodbyes to be said: "*Auf Wiedersetien!*"

•••

Another ski season was starting, and although there had not been much snow we knew that situation could change overnight.

A colleague of Kurt's, a Scot he had worked with at Watson Lake, had recently married and his wife enjoyed skiing, so they had asked to come up to Whistler for a visit. Bob had not said when they would arrive that weekend, so we went out to the cabin early to prepare for our guests. As there was too little snow on the lower slopes (and too many stumps sticking out) we decided to go helicopter skiing on the mountaintop, and I decided to take a few lessons from Trude. When we returned, we were pleased to see our guests had arrived and were waiting for us. Bob's wife, Vera was beautiful: tall, slim and dark. We welcomed them and showed them to their room just as our friends started arriving.

"We thought it would be nicer here than at the L'Aprés," they said. "The *gemuetlichkeit* is missing over there and besides, it's too crowded."

The men immediately surrounded Vera; Kurt built a fire and I sliced some sausage while Branko opened a bottle of his home brew and Stan delivered the latest jokes.

The conversation drifted from one topic to another, until the subject was Indians – their latest demands, their rights, and Indians in general. Some called them lazy, others said there was more bad than good about the race. Everyone had an opinion except Vera, who sat quietly. Eventually the person sitting next to her said, "How do you feel about the Indians, Vera?" and she replied, so quietly, "I am a Native person."

There was a complete, shocked silence, broken eventually by Vera laughing, "Don't worry, I won't scalp you! But I would like to straighten out a few things." Nobody could believe she was a full-blooded Indian, this tall, lovely girl; but in our embarrassment, rather then begin a possible argument by having Vera dispute our comments earlier, we changed the subject. Leo started the music, and the men practically fought for the chance to dance with Vera. It was not guilty consciences alone that prompted their eagerness! I was amazed at how well she danced the polkas and waltzes we preferred, and was anxious to see her ski. Skiing was not a sport the Indians seemed to enjoy, for I'd never before seen an Indian on the slopes. Vera protested that she was not a very good skier, which simply made us all want to teach her.

The next day we spent more time sitting in the Roundhouse than in skiing. Somebody was pounding the piano, heavy on the bass, and "It sounds like an Indian war dance," I commented to Vera thoughtlessly. But she agreed, and on the way down in the gondola both she and Bob said what a lovely time they had had.

Just as they were preparing to leave, Vera ran out to the car and returned carrying an enormous bearskin – a grizzly bear skin! "You must accept this for your hospitality," she insisted. "I shot it myself."

We thanked her, thinking that certainly here was the proof of her roots. We invited them to visit again soon, and they promised they would. We added, "Next time, you don't have to bring us a bear; you can bring some beer!"

As we drove back to Vancouver, Kurt asked, "Did you hear what Bob was saying? There are more jobs in Alberta than here." Bob was an engineer and traveled a great deal, so I was sure this information was correct. "Things are not good here any more," Kurt continued. "I estimated twenty jobs recently, and got no contracts from it." Kurt seldom discussed his business problems with me, and when he did I knew it had reached a critical point. "I will try Alberta," he said now, "especially if I should get the Fort St. John job I estimated."

"What is that job?"

"An observation tower. And after that, there may be something coming up in Grande Prairie."

"Where is Grande Prairie?"

"Agnes, don't you remember that when we went to the prairies we stayed there overnight and you liked it. It's near Edmonton."

"Oh, *ja*. Are we moving to Alberta then?"

"No, we will just set up an office and maybe rent a house. Kurt Jr. would probably move up for a while."

We got the Fort St. John job, and the one in Grande Prairie too. The two projects were not too far distant from one another, but the pressure of traveling back and forth between them began to tell and I worried about Kurt's health. There were no more relaxing weekends on Whistler, just traveling between the two towns.

As his father had surmised, Kurt Jr. moved to Grande Prairie and I packed extra winter clothes for both men, as it was getting quite cold there.

I hoped to go north to give Kurt Jr. a hand setting up the house; he was still so young! Eventually I did go, and wound up taking over the cooking for the family and the camp workers. Meanwhile, Vivian ran the office in Vancouver.

The Alberta situation at that time was many jobs, few workers, little accommodation. Often we had to hire men from Vancouver and then find them housing at the jobsite, no easy task. How different from Vancouver! Many times we had to stop work because of the weather (the temperature would drop to thirty-five below zero) which we certainly had never done in Vancouver.

Our Christmas holidays were shorter than usual, and for the first time in many years, were not spent on Whistler, skiing, which Kurt missed most of all.

It was inevitable.

A third heart attack.

No one was surprised, particularly not the doctor. He informed Kurt that he would not be able to work for at least three weeks once he was out of the hospital, which made Kurt quite angry. "I can't afford that!" he stormed. "Whether you can or not, you have no other choice. You have go to slow down, take it easy," the doctor advised.

I was so glad when Kurt was out of the Intensive Care Unit – that section of the hospital was so frightening, with the screens showing each heartbeat as you sit visiting. Not so bad when the lines are stable, but when they leap and dance on the monitors it is difficult to maintain a calm pose for the patient!

In his private room, Kurt told me to make the necessary preparations, for we were going to Europe.

"When are we going?" I asked.

"In February, with Doug," he replied. He had obviously been doing a lot of thinking as he lay there, inactive for once. "And I'll tell you another thing. I am thinking about retiring. It is not worth it anymore. We'll buy a house on Whistler. I am really tired...."

"But there is no doctor at Whistler," I thought. I did not like the idea of retiring on Whistler; it was too isolated from medical facilities Kurt might need. But I thought he might find another spot he would like as well, and left hoping that. As I was going out the door, Kurt called after me, "Bring me some bread. The bread they get here is not even good enough to plaster walls!" The nurse overheard this and smiled. They had gotten used to Kurt here.

• • •

After Kurt recovered we went up to Grande Prairie again, but by this time it was summer on the prairies. The cold and snow had vanished and wild roses were blooming in their place. It was strange how everything here reminded me so much of my early childhood – the smell of flowers, the women with their kerchiefs. "Can we move up here and retire?" I asked hopefully. "It's so peaceful, not so much hustle and bustle. Small towns are never so hectic."

"That's why we go to Whistler," Kurt said.

Our son greeted us when we arrived, and I lost no time telling him how much I liked the countryside there.

"I am missing trees," he replied. "They have absolutely no trees up here. But that's good for the hot air balloon competition which they are preparing for."

While father and son toured the jobsites, I watched the townspeople and listened to their dialects. There were Polish, Ukrainian, and Hungarian immigrants, and something I had not noticed on previous visits caught my eyes: they walked side by side with the Indians, chatting freely. Maybe it was something that was common in other places, and after our experience with Vera I had become more sensitive to it.

As soon as the men were finished we went to our own Little House on the Prairie. It was nice enough, but if it were not for a big stone in front I would not have been able to tell it from the other houses on that street. Our landlord, hearing we were in town, came by for a visit, bringing me a huge bunch of Prairie flowers. I offered him coffee and we chatted away. He came from Switzerland many years ago, working first in Vancouver as a pastry chef at the Hotel Vancouver until, as he put it, "it got too crazy down there." Then he moved to Grande Prairie and had been happy there ever since. "I own eight houses," he told us proudly.

"That's quite an achievement," I said. "But did you never want to go back to Switzerland? Did you not miss the mountains?"

"No. My wife did, but not me."

I asked if he would mind if I planted a few flowers, as the yard was so bare. "The grass is nice and green this year," I noticed. "Usually the grass gets so brown on the prairies." It does not rain as much here as in Vancouver, but when it does rain it is short and intense, and the air is so fresh afterwards. There are many more thunderstorms, and it looked as though one was brewing just then. Suddenly a strong wind arose, scattering everything outdoors, including some lumber that had been piled in front of the house. I called to Kurt and some workmen to come help me collect all that lumber.

Kurt Jr. laughed, "Do you still want to move up here, Mum?"

•••

We watched the balloon competition on the weekend and it was quite a show, with all colours represented on the balloons themselves. The weather co-operated; the sky was blue and the sun was playing with all those colours. "It must be nice to be up there," I thought, "floating free and high." I remembered the times I had thought that same thing when I flew my kite, when I was a child in Austria.

Our business finished, we headed back to Vancouver, by truck as we were hauling some materials. I worried about Kurt's health and the effect driving over a thousand miles would have, but he assured me he felt fine. We stopped a number of times, including a respite at Stuart Lake so Kurt and Erhardt could do some hunting, and at Fort St. John to check the progress of the tower there.

It was an indian summer; pleasant days, but cool mornings and evenings. At the Fort St. John jobsite I noticed Kurt nervously smoking cigarette after cigarette and wondered if there was something wrong. Of course, since the doctor had advised him that if he must smoke, to smoke only half the cigarette to minimize the tar and nicotine taken in, Kurt didn't smoke whole cigarettes now. He finished his packs off more quickly, and his habit cost more, but it did seem to be healthier.

We ate lunch with the foreman, and he told us he had bagged a moose the previous week, so Kurt was more interested than ever in taking a hunting trip with Erhardt.

We went on; Kurt tired easily, as he was the only driver, I couldn't manage the truck, and also occasionally forgot to take his medication. By the time we reached Prince George we were quite worn out, but glad to see Ushi and Erhardt, and they were happy to receive us.

The next day, the four of us drove up to Stuart Lake. As it was too cold for swimming now, Ushi and I went for a walk while the men prepared their hunting gear. We met some neighbours on our walk, and as we strolled we noticed a young woman who seemed a little lost. In the course of our conversation with her, we discovered that she was waiting for a group who had gone out in a boat but had not yet returned. "Don't worry," said Ushi, "if they aren't back by nightfall, you can spend the night with us."

We discovered the woman's name was Tina, and that she was a coronary nurse. I was so pleased! "May I call on you if my husband gets sick?" I asked. "He just came out of the hospital not too long ago, after having his third heart attack. I worry about him; he shouldn't smoke, but..."

"Don't worry about his smoking," Tina said. "With heart patients we have found the frustration of not having a cigarette is harder for them and offsets the health benefits of not smoking. But certainly, call on me any time if you need me."

As we were leaving, I asked again, "May I call on you, even at night?"

"Yes, Yes, any time!" she assured me.

Afterwards, Ushi asked me, "What is the matter with you? Are you expecting trouble?"

"No, but I like to be prepared," I replied.

Kurt and Erhardt were rolling up their sleeping bags; they had cleaned their guns and seemed ready for a morning departure. Ushi heated up some stew for dinner and served her homemade cheesecake for dessert. I watched disapprovingly as Kurt had a second and then a third piece. Really, he should not have had any; the doctor warned him that he had too much sugar in his blood. But that was Kurt. He never did what the doctor or anybody else told him to.

Later, neighbours came visiting, and we had fish talk: everyone had caught the biggest fish, and as the numbers and lengths increased the longer they talked it was quite a relief when one of the fishermen, who was also a skier, turned the subject from fish to skis. Now Kurt took over the conversation, telling them about his skiing in the war. "We did not ski for pleasure, then. It was serious business."

"How did you manage to carry your equipment, guns and all?" asked someone. "I have a hard time balancing myself on skis, without carrying anything."

"Well, the ski patrol does it all the time, carrying people on stretchers. I guess it's tougher when you have someone like my wife."

Now everyone looked in my direction.

"I went on a diet after that experience!" I said.

"Why did they carry you down the mountain? Did you break

your leg?"

"She had two broken legs," Kurt said.

The man next to Kurt returned the conversation to the war. "What did they call those army skiers? They had a name."

"The *Gebirsjaeger*," Kurt said. I asked Erhardt to translate this for us, and he said it meant "Mountainhunters."

"You must be a good hunter as well as a good skier," remarked one lady.

"In Europe a lot of people use their skis not only for pleasure. The milkmen, the mailmen, the police and the army use skis."

Erhardt kept filling our glasses with wine and we carried on talking 'till the Northern Lights took the stage and escorted us to our sleeping quarters.

I woke up later to hear someone wandering around the cabin. At first I assumed it was one of the guests still here, but it was Kurt. "What is the matter? Why can't you sleep?"

"I have pains."

"Pains? Where?"

"In my chest," he said calmly.

"Oh, my God." Now I was wide-awake, and so were Ushi and Erhardt. I immediately put on a coat and ran into the windy night calling "Tina! Tina!" so loudly that I woke up the whole neighbourhood.

Where was her boat? Where was she?

Finally, she heard me calling and came with pills for Kurt. "You must wait until morning to move him. It would be too rough by boat or car just now. Does anyone here have a telephone?"

Nobody did. I had once thought how nice it was to be cut off from the world, but right now it was a nightmare.

It seemed morning would never come. I couldn't sleep, but Kurt dozed; perhaps the pills had helped. Without bothering with breakfast we drove to the hospital in Fort St. James, where the doctor examined Kurt immediately. Unable to determine if it had been another heart attack, he asked Kurt to remain for observation and asked if he had ever had a heart attack before.

"He seems to get them like other people get colds," Erhardt said.

Kurt fought the idea of staying at the hospital, but Erhardt calmed him down and promised to bring our gear from the cabin and drop it off on their way back to Prince George. Meanwhile, I took a room at a nearby hotel, which was in easy walking distance from the hospital. When not in the hospital, I walked around the village of Fort St. James, noticing the mixed white and Native population, the shops, the hotels and the helicopter pad I had overlooked on previous visits.

Kurt was complaining about hospital food again, a sure sign he was getting better, I thought. He was still hooked up to the monitor, which was outside his room in the corridor. I assumed this was because there was no intensive care unit.

"Why can't I go home?" Kurt kept asking. "I have been here seventeen days now and they still don't know. I tell you, I'm okay!"

"Take it easy, Kurt," I would say.

"You and your 'take it easy.' If it were that simple, I would take it easy. I can't just quit everything right now; besides, I will have to drive that truck back."

"We'll fly back. Erhardt will take care of the truck."

As I walked back to the hotel, I wondered if stress really was the reason people get heart attacks. In Kurt's case, the culprit seemed to be sugar. Every time his sugar level went up, he would have another heart attack – and he had had three pieces of Ushi's cake the evening before his last attack. Life is hectic for us all, though it was so different from when I was younger. In my little Austrian village we used to walk everywhere and on the weekend we would go hunting and fishing, though we did not have to drive a thousand miles to enjoy these sports. Certainly we were not usually successful, and rarely caught a fish, but it was a nice, easy way of life. I wondered if the Natives, with their seemingly less-hectic lifestyle, had the same rate of heart attacks.

Kurt was in hospital three weeks before he was released. He was eventually diagnosed as having pleurisy; the doctor said he could have killed himself if he had gone hunting in his condition, even if his heart hadn't been troubling him already.

It took no time to get back into the old routine once back in Vancouver. Up early for work, joining the crowds – neighbours, friends all engaged in the same rat race. There is no way out, and we were lucky to have Whistler to retreat to for a few days at a time.

"Thank God," Kurt would say on arrival at the cabin. "At last."

But why was he showing me a pamphlet on Squaw Valley now?

"How would you like to go there this Christmas, with the kids too?"

"But I thought the doctor said you should take it easy?"

"With work, not with holidays."

"Will you promise not to ski there?"

"Of course I will ski there. Why would I go there if I'm not going to ski?"

I didn't like to argue with Kurt those days, so I suggested Mount Hood instead, if he was so determined to ski. It would be closer if Kurt were to get sick again. But – "Look at the brochure," he said as he left for work.

I could see why Kurt was attracted. "Site of the 1960 Olympic Games!" read the brochure. "European-style skiing from November until July! Located in California's High Sierra." Look at the length of those lifts! Red Dog Double Lift is five thousand feet – almost a mile! Where did they get those names? KT-22 sounds like it should be ridden by secret agents! But reading about the resort gave me goose pimples and I really wished we could go somewhere else; I couldn't imagine skiing those runs. Maybe Kurt will change his mind and just want to go to Whistler again – if Squaw Valley is Kurt's idea of a Christmas present, I don't want it! I regretted ever complaining about our habitual weekend trips to Whistler; at least I knew the runs.

We did go to Whistler for the weekend with a little delay en route as there had been a rockslide near Porteau Cove on the Squamish highway. We were told there would be a two-hour wait until it was cleared, and although I suggested we turn back, Kurt wouldn't dream of it. So it was late when we arrived at Whistler, and dark; dark streets (no lights yet), dark houses (not too many people here this time of year, when it is too late for swimming and too early for skiing). Still, Kurt always finds something to do: paint the house, cut the grass. This time he planned to fix the balcony, and was also trying to figure out if he had enough room to build a sauna.

We woke up to a light dusting of the first snow of the season – not enough to ski, but enough to make a skier's heart race. I was always happy to see the first snow of the season, and hoped that if we had a lot of snow here, Kurt might not want to got to Squaw Valley.

We did get quite a bit more snow, and some weeks later Kurt and I walked across fresh, cold powder early one Saturday, to the Gondola. Our house was within easy walking distance, which was a convenience for many of our friends, who would be unable to find parking in the lot and so would leave their vehicles at our place and walk from there.

It was early morning, which was one of my favourite times to ski for then we avoided the crowd. Better to go up early and come down early than to come down with the thousands of other skiers all coming down at the same time. That was like rush hour on the Lion's Gate Bridge, only without a policeman to control it; people would just yell and if one didn't jump in time, they'd ski right over you and continue on their way – an alpine hit and run.

Today there was already a long lineup, but none of our friends were here yet so Kurt would have to ski with me. I was pleased with the arrangement, for with me there was no competition and he could take it easy, which he should anyway.

And as bonus, I'd get a ski lesson for free!

It was snowing all the way up and I remembered the Native saying: Little snow, big snow; big snow, little snow, which means little flakes mean a lot of snow and big flakes mean a little snow. Right now we had a lot of little flakes and everyone was wearing goggles except me. They gave me claustrophobia.

I am always a little nervous skiing with Kurt; he is so critical. Not that he would hit me with a ski pole for some error but he just couldn't understand how someone could make so many ski turns so terribly slowly. "Well, that's my specialty," I say.

"BED ZEE KNEES," we hear behind us – but it was not meant for us; it was the French instructor from the ski school talking to one of his pupils.

Up and down we go, and each time the lineup for the lift gets longer. It seemed everyone was skiing the Green chair today, so we decided to move over to Olympic. But Olympic did not have enough snow yet and we returned to Green. As we were riding up the lift, we spotted Midge below us, schussing down. "For an English girl, she skis pretty good," Kurt remarked, his eyes following her.

Later we caught sight of Branko and skied toward him. He offered us a drink from his flask, which had the dual effect of warming me up and giving me some extra courage so that I skied much better, and faster. In fact, I was doing so well I decided to ask Branko for another sip from his flask. People did not bother me anymore; neither did the moguls or trees and as I flashed past Kurt I just smiled at him as he yelled at me to "keep those legs together!" Other times I would have been embarrassed to have the whole mountain hear us, but today nothing bothered me.

The next day Vivian arrived with a few friends and Kurt Jr. dropped in too. We had a day of family skiing and afterwards, showed some home movies.

"Who is that with the funny knickers?" asked Vivian's friend.

"That's my dad."

"Is that at Whistler?"

"No, it's at Mount Baker," I said. "Look, there you are Vivian, with your first skis; pretty good downhill," (at this point, Kurt ran the film backwards) "and just as good going uphill!"

"Now comes Whistler," Kurt announced. "Watch now, this is in the West Bowl where Mum broke her leg."

"Who is that fantastic skier?" asked the young people.

"That's Helmut," Kurt and I said together. "He skied like a god."

Everyone was just agreeing to this when the film ended and Trude walked in, too late to see our film of her late husband and perhaps it was just as well.

At this point we decided we'd seen enough films, the young people left to visit friends and Kurt, Trude and I sat and talked. Trude told us there was another art exhibition scheduled soon, with home baking as well as the usual craft and art displays and sale. We were just arranging to meet her there when we had more company arrive; this time, Jim and Barbara, our American friends. Barbara worked in a ski shop and so these two were always in the latest ski fashions – it was a delight to see what new outfit they'd be sporting this year!

Jim and Barbara invited us for supper, and by the time we had finished visiting, practicing the latest ski turns and enjoying the latest music it was midnight before we sat down to eat. We decided to put those new turns into practice on the slopes the following day, which reminded Kurt that "Agnes was skiing very well 'gesterday,' after she had some of Branko's Schnapps."

It was really cold as we walked back to our cabin, and I said, "It will be icy tomorrow."

"Don't get scared already, now," Kurt said as he hugged me. "You can always go in the Roundhouse if you don't like it."

As it turned out, it was not icy at all, as families and friends skied together. In fact, everyone spent so much time in the clear mountain air that they were quite tired at the end of the day, and it was early evening all round, for once.

Kurt had a meeting in town the following day, and we left early to avoid the heavy traffic. At home, we found an invitation from one of our neighbours pinned to our door – for a Christmas party and carol singing!

"So early?" Kurt asked.

"They want to start practicing the carols, I think. That's why the early invitation. What do you think, shall we go?"

Kurt was hesitant, and I knew why. We had had bad experiences with parties in other neighbourhoods. We had been invited, all right, but once there, they had started singing old German marching songs and with us being the only Austrians, it was obvious.

When we first arrived in this neighbourhood, it was like a little British colony, but now had more of an international flavour, with Swedes, Danes, Icelandics, and more Germans and Austrians. Canada is such a big country; was it intended only for the Natives, or for all of us? There is room for all on this earth, if only we share. Share and care.

"Let's go," I said to Kurt. "We'll go to the party, but skip the carol singing."

That early invitation reminded me it was time to start planning for Christmas myself – to get the parcels and cards off to Europe, especially. This year too, I though, it would be nice to decorate our house outside like everyone else.

"Do you think we could have lights outside?" I asked. "And maybe some decoration in the window?"

"What do you have in mind?" Kurt asked.

"You know what would look nice? Stenciled figurers on the windows of the whole Christmas story; lit from the inside, it would form a silhouette."

"You and your ideas!" Kurt said indulgently. "I'll see what I can do, and if I have enough time, I'll do it."

When Christmas arrived it was all done and turned out a masterpiece. All the neighbours liked it too, as they informed us when they came carol singing. "Why did you not come with us?" they asked.

"Somebody has to stay home to listen," Kurt answered, and they all laughed.

"But will you come over later?" asked the couple whose invitation had welcomed us back from Whistler some weeks before.

We went, as we had said we would, and found practically the whole neighbourhood gathered there, old-timers as well as new arrivals we had not met yet. Someone handed us a drink, and in keeping with the friendly atmosphere, told us "When that's gone, just help yourselves. The bar is open."

As I looked around and admired the decorations I noted that their tree was decorated mostly in red; rising almost to the ceiling. It was very dramatic. I was used to mostly white, gold and silver on a tree but thought I too would try a red theme next year.

As was customary at this time of year, the colour scheme of most of the ladies' dresses was green or red, and there I was in white. I supposed next year, I would have a red tree and a red dress, too.

While we were chatting with a couple we had not met before, the carol singers arrived and then it was standing room only; but nobody minded. The hostess announced that the buffet was ready (set up in the corner of the room, the table was decorated with holly and pine boughs – very festive)! We were all to help ourselves. The food was plentiful, and you'd have thought they were entertaining the U.N. – English pudding, German stolen, Hungarian shortbread, and Swedish smorgasbord. But we got an even bigger surprise at the bar, for in addition to the usual whisky, gin and vodka there was German wine and every kind of beer including Austrian Steffl beer. Since Kurt was the only one who drank that, we were really moved. They had got that in just for us.

We sang along to carol accompaniment by the piano, and I did not mind a bit when they tried to sing *O Tannenbaum* in German.

"It was nice," I said to Kurt as we walked home, and he nodded.

At home, I wrapped a few presents while Kurt made us each a drink, and then we sat quietly, enjoying our drinks and our tree that was lit with the electric candles we had bought on Robsonstrasse. They looked so real, and so lovely reflected in the glass skylight. I turned to remind Kurt to set the alarm for morning and saw he had fallen asleep, with a smile on his face.

Chapter Eighteen
Europe – Once More, with Feeling!

New Year's Eve we had our traditional phone call from Doug and Laural. "Happy New Year! Are we still going to Europe?" asked Doug.

"Wait, I'll call Kurt." When he took the phone from me, Kurt had his usual joke.

"Hello, Father Douglas. *Ja*, this year is the year. You'd better get ready, we don't have that much time anymore. We are getting older. How about February? Construction is slow then."

After Kurt had hung up, I asked, "Are we really going?"

"I told you we are. Why don't you believe me?"

I believed him, and immediately started looking for our passports. "We need new passports," I called. Kurt just laughed.

"I need two hours to pack," he said. "You need two months to get ready!"

"That's right, and I do have exactly two months. It's not like going to Whistler or Prince George, you know."

"Okay. If that's how you have fun, you can start packing tomorrow, but right now let's have a glass of champagne for the New Year. It will be fun to go with Doug and Laural and show them our country." They had helped us so much in our new country; I could not think of anybody I would rather go with.

We listened to all the news and weather reports from the old country now, and discovered Germany was in the midst of a deep freeze; in fact, the army had had to come in to remove the snow. I hoped Doug and Laural had been following the reports and would take lots of warm clothing.

I brushed up on my history and geography, for surely they would have lots of questions and I didn't want to give the wrong answers.

•••

Off to Europe! We boarded the big jumbo jet at Vancouver with mixed feelings – sad to say goodbye to our children, but happy to see our homeland once more.

Doug and Laural joined us in Calgary, dressed in ski outfits. We had said we would ski in Europe, and it looked as though they could hardly wait.

The long flight was broken up by meals, naps and those free airline drinks, and before we could find out who the murderer was in that old Hitchcock film they were showing, we were touching down in Amsterdam.

The news of the cold snap in Europe was not exaggerated. The snow was deep and the cold wind whipped around the people dressed in fur coats and hats. There were no wooden shoes being worn today!

On our way to customs, we noticed Doug had disappeared and, feeling responsible for him, searched everywhere – washrooms, coffee shops – until we spotted him coming toward us, his hands full of things he had just bought.

"Have you ever been here before?" we asked.

"No, never."

"Then let's try to stick together for now."

We flagged down a taxi and headed for the hotel where we had reserved rooms.

"They don't seem very friendly," Doug remarked as a sour-looking hotel clerk handed us the necessary forms to complete.

"What did you expect? This isn't Arnheim."

We were planning a side trip to that town which had been liberated by Canadian soldiers during the Second World War. Laural's brother, who had been killed in that action, was buried near there and she hoped to find his grave.

We told Doug not to let the clerk's behaviour bother him – he was probably too young to remember the Liberation. We decided to dress for dinner, and were half-way through our preparations when Doug rushed in from his room, wondering why the electricity had gone off.

"I was just shaving," he said, "and the power went off."

Kurt looked at the razor which Doug was still holding – his electric model from Canada. As the outlets in Europe are not equipped to accommodate North American appliances, an adaptor is needed and Doug had neglected to notice this. He had knocked out the power in his suite as a result! After that, Doug shaved with a regular safety razor.

As we passed the desk, we said to the clerk, "By the time we get back, we'd like to have the light fixed in our room – it doesn't seem to work."

The clerk apologized as we hurried off, trying hard to keep from laughing.

The following day we picked up a car from the rental agency and decided to pack all our suitcases in it. Kurt drove and Doug was appointed navigator, though I wondered if he would be familiar enough with the signs to give directions. The streets in and around Amsterdam were treacherous as we left early that morning. It looked like we had hit the rush hour; there were a few cars piled up beside the road but our car was in good shape and Kurt was doing his best. Visibility was quite bad.

Doug gave a couple of wrong directions, then in frustration asked, "How many places do they have here with the name '*Einfahrt*'?"

"'*Einfahrt*' is not the name of a village," we explained. "'*Einfahrt*' means 'Enter' and '*Ausfahrt*' means 'Exit'." I could see not understanding the language could pose a great difficulty.

I had a bad cold and kept blowing my nose; eventually, it got to be too much for Laural, she had been watching for windmills. "Don't you have a Kleenex?" she asked.

"No," I said. "I use a handkerchief."

"Handkerchief? That's old fashioned," she scoffed.

"We had handkerchiefs in Europe before we came to Canada and what's wrong with a handkerchief, anyway?" My cold was making me feel peevish.

"Everything," she shot back.

Doug tried to pacify us: "You use handkerchiefs, we use Kleenex," he said.

"Oh, shut-up about handkerchiefs and Kleenex," Kurt yelled. "Look! There's a windmill!"

"You watch the road and never mind about windmills, or we'll wind up in a ditch!" I yelled back.

"And look at all the tulips," Doug said.

"Tulips? Under the snow? Doug, you better look at the map and not for tulips. Tell me where I have to turn."

"What are we looking for?"

"Utrecht."

"What's at Utrecht?"

"A university. But we're not going to Utrecht, just making a turn there."

"There is a sign. Can you see it? Utrecht ahead."

We always argued like that, more for fun than in anger.

After driving a while we stopped at a restaurant; more friendly here, they helped us with the menu. The food was not all that good, but not all that bad either. The coffee was too strong for Doug and Laural's taste, but I loved it.

"I am entitled to an opinion!" Doug replied.

This was going to be fun – criticizing, analyzing; I thought we would be seeing Europe as never before, and looked forward to it.

The struggle with Dutch place names continued, and in despair Kurt took the map from Doug and studied it.

"Why don't we just ask someone?" I demanded.

"Do you speak Dutch?" replied Laural.

"We go left," Kurt announced, and after a while we knew he was right as we arrived in Arnheim.

The big cemetery was covered with snow and we could hardly read the names on the crosses. There was so much sadness here; we all became silent. I reached for Laural's arm and together we wandered over a battle-field from yesterday. "How strange," I thought. "Our brothers fought against each other, but today it makes no difference."

After this interlude, we drove to the German border and realized that the reports of heavy snowfalls in Germany had not been exaggerated. The army was out clearing but driving was still tough. We had snow tires on our car, but really needed chains.

As the place names got too difficult for Doug, he took over driving while Kurt directed. "Just follow the River Rhine," he joked.

We decided to stop and take pictures, and have a snack somewhere.

"You would not know they had a war here," Laural was saying. "Where are all the ruins? I guess they cleaned up just for us!"

"You know, it is just about Carnival time in Cologne," Kurt mentioned. "We'll be just in time."

"I would never have thought that *Koeln* stands for Cologne. They should keep place names international."

We stopped at a German Inn where Kurt and I had sauerkraut. I thought the smell might bother people who don't like sauerkraut, but Doug and Laural liked the stuff now. When our orders came, we asked the proprietor for directions and he told us we were not far from the East German border.

"The East German border!" we all echoed. "We don't want to go there! We'd like to go to Koeln!"

"Ah, Köln!" the man said.

"*Ja,*" said Doug, pretending he spoke German.

"Where do you come from?" the man inquired curiously.

"From Canada!"

Pointing at Kurt and me he said, "But you are not from Canada, are you?"

"Well, not originally."

"Do people eat sauerkraut there, too?"

"Oh, *ja*. We get everything there."

It was around noon when we arrived in Cologne. Everybody was in a joyous mood, wandering the streets all dressed up for the Carnival. There was singing and dancing, but we decided to find a place to stay before we joined the merry makers. It was more difficult than we had imagined – every hotel was booked solid. Tired and hungry from our searching, we decided to change our money for German marks at a nearby bank. As we walked in the door, the manager and staff greeted us with a glass of wine and "*Prost!*" We soon found we couldn't get any money at the banks today, just wine. Nobody works as "It is *'Fasching'*." The manager asked where we were from and when we told him, he said if we came back the following day he'd change our money. "Where are you staying?" he asked.

"Actually, nowhere. We haven't been able to find a place yet."

"Go down to the Hotel Adler and have your lunch there; it's a good place. Ask for the manager there and say I sent you. He'll give you a room. It might be his own, but you don't mind that, do you?"

The hotel Adler was also booked solid, but the manager did give us his private suite; we wondered where he would sleep that night.

"I guess they don't sleep here in *Fasching*," Kurt said.

The hotel was within walking distance of the cathedral, the famous *Koelner Dom* with its two steeples, and we decided to get a closer look at it and say a prayer before joining in the celebrations. Others had had the same idea, and had come in costume – clowns and knights joined us there, and eve Till Eulenspiegel said a prayer. We seemed the only ones not properly dressed.

The church was beautiful, with no sign of where the bombs had raged through it. "They sure did a good cleanup job on this," Doug remarked as we entered the cold dark church from the blinding sunshine.

The streets were full of people having one big party, and we wished we had the time to spend a few days. But as our time was limited, we had to move on in order to see as much as possible.

After Cologne it was historic Nuremberg. While driving there we talked about the Nuremberg Trial and got to wondering about the name of the American judge at that trial. We decided to stop at Bratwurstgloekerl, a famous inn. We asked if anyone knew the judge's name. Nobody knew, and it seemed nobody cared. "Why do you want to know?" somebody asked. "It happened such a long time ago. We didn't understand it then and we don't want to know or talk about it now." And he went on with his meal.

Our lunch was very pleasing, and we had beer in a huge *stein*. I said to Doug, "My brother will know. We will ask him the judge's name when we arrive in Salzburg." After purchasing *Lebkuchen* to take along, we headed Munich.

"I will take over the driving and navigation. I'm at home here," Kurt said.

"What about Heidelberg?" Laural asked. "I'd like to see that old university there."

"I'd rather go to Dachau," Doug said, his fingers pointing out other sites of interest on the map.

"We'll need three years to see all that, and you still want to go skiing," I said. "Let's just continue to Munich and Salzburg – Kurt's and Mozart's birthplace."

In Munich there was building going on everywhere, and detour signs wherever we tried to drive. It looked as though they were rebuilding the whole road system by detours. We arrived at the famous Hofbrauehaus; what tourist would skip the opportunity to have a beer there? Kurt and Doug were no exception. Laural and I, however, decided to do a little shopping; it was not long before we realized we should have brought the men with us, for everything was expensive and the shopping money they had given us was not enough for so much as a handkerchief.

"Look at all those fur coats in the window!" Laural exclaimed.

"*Ja*, but look at all the fur coats the people are wearing!"

"Walking up and down the streets like a bunch of show-offs," she said.

Once again I felt I had to defend my European heritage. "It's no more showing off than the people in Vancouver driving to the Queen Elizabeth Theatre all dressed up in fur coats, then leaving them in the coat check during the performance. People there don't need those coats but here, people walk outdoors and it's cold."

Doug came up and said, "Don't you two start again. Why don't you look for a fur jacket here, Laural? You wanted to buy one anyway."

Did you look at the prices?" she said. "I'd much rather buy a ski out-fit."

"Well, let's look for that, then."

"I think you'll find better in Salzburg. I know all the shops there and they have a good selection," I said.

As we drove the *Autobahn* toward Salzburg, we could see the mountains in the background.

"This was one of Hitler's good ideas," Doug said.

"What??"

"The *Autobahn*. By the way, where is the Eagle's Nest?'

That's in Berchtesgaden, and we thought we might be able to go there. But we still wanted to go skiing, and visit Vienna and Wiener Neustadt.

It was thirty years ago since I marched with my parents all the way to Badgastein from Wiener Neustadt. "Imagine," Kurt said. "I would never have met you if it was not for that war."

"How far is it to Salzburg?"

"Just around the corner," Kurt said and I wondered if he felt as I did? My heart was pounding faster at the sight of the familiar things. After all, this city of *The Sound of Music* had once been home.

In the distance, we could see Hohensalzburg, perched high up on the hill. The mountains were covered in snow and so were the streets. The people in loden coats and Salzburg hats were walking everywhere; every-thing was the same as it had been when we left. There was no need for change here; everything had been finished a long time ago and there was no need for new things. In fact, the Salzburg Cathedral is over one thou-sand years old, and I pointed it out to Doug and Laural as it came into view.

"It's not like North American cities," I said. "There they are still build-ing and changing. People here have no desire to change this. They like it the way it is."

Our first stop was to visit Kurt's mother. Living all alone in a four-plex, she is quite lonely now that all her children have scattered around the world. There was her familiar face looking out the window at us, and her voice calling, "*Ja, ich komme!*" in response to our ring.

Doug and Laural spoke no German and Kurt's mother spoke no English, but there is an unspoken language of welcome; no words were needed to see her greet her son and go all out to please everybody. I noticed her hands were shaking as she handed out the coffee and home-made cake (Kurt's favourite).

We had chosen a hotel about halfway between my family's home and Kurt's mother's, a place where we had stayed on our last trip to Salzburg. It was within easy walking distance of everything, and since walking is usually faster than driving in Salzburg anyway, we were quite happy with it and Doug and Laural were pleased with our choice as well.

After washing and unpacking we were off to see my brother, Fritz, and his family who were waiting for us. Doug and Laural must have been relieved that he spoke English, for they had been speaking mostly to us alone on the trip. It must have been good to speak to someone else for a change.

"Gasoline sure is expensive here," Doug said.

"*Ja.* The people here drive only on Sundays. They keep their cars pol-ished and in the garage."

"With these prices, I don't blame them."

We asked Fritz about skiing and he suggested a place and offered to make reservations for us, asking when we wanted to go. When we said we hoped to ski the following day, he said in astonishment, "Tomorrow!"

"*Ja*, we haven't all that much time. We still want to see Vienna, Venice..." said Kurt.

"Just make reservations for three, Fritz," I said. "I will stay in Salzburg. I want to visit the cemetery, and Kurt's mother as well. We can't just come and say 'hello, goodbye' to her. And you know I am not all that crazy about skiing."

Next day, before the ski expedition, we went shopping in Getreidegasse and found Laural a ski suit. Getredegasse is the same street on which stands the house in which Mozart was born, and we showed Doug and Laural that, then showed them where Kurt and I had worked, where Kurt went to school and where we had been married. Then it was time for the skiers to leave on their trip, which would keep them away for two days. In the meantime, I planned to visit old friends and family.

The two days passed quickly and the skiers returned, satisfied except for Kurt. His equipment was not the best, and he had not skied as well as he had wanted to as a result. "Just an excuse," said Laural, "because I skied better."

"I don't care how I skied," Doug remarked. "I'm just happy to have skied in the birthplace of downhill skiing! And did you hear them all talking there about 'Lech'? It's supposed to be out of this world!"

"Maybe we can get there," Kurt said, "But I have still to visit my mother and also my brother in Graz. You figure out in the meantime if you want to go to Venice or Paris or if you want to go skiing again. We can't make both." So we left them to work out the itinerary and went to drop off a few things at Fritz'. By the time we got back, Doug had figured it all out – "First to Innsbruck, then down to Italy, back to Graz via Yugoslavia – isn't that where your brother is? Or, we got first to Venice and do it the other way around.

"Let me see the map," said Kurt. "I think you've got it all mixed up."

While the men were checking over the map, Laural and I started packing. "Don't tell me where we are going," she said. "I want to be surprised."

And surprised she was in finding herself in Venice, Italy. Venice was warmer than any place we had been so far, and was such a romantic place. We found a nice little *pansion*, with fountains and statues in the garden. The lady who ran the *pansion* told us in broken English that it had been her home once, but she is now a widow and must take in guests. "I am sure she must have had servants," I thought, as she served us cold drinks and pretzels. Even the pretzels were heart-shaped; it is Valentine's Day here all year. After registering, we drove out sightseeing, first to the Cathedral, eventually ending up on St. Mark Place feeding the pigeons. We sat for a while in a sidewalk café, then decided we had to take a ride in a gondola. That is a must in Venice! The romance sours a little by the smell in some of the canals but we overlooked that. We saw Doug and Laural in their gondola but before we could take a picture they disappeared behind a big palace.

"Does anyone still live there?" we asked our gondolier.

"Yes, sometimes," he replied.

One day is not really enough to see all Venice, but we had to go on. As we were eating our spaghetti Kurt asked, "How would you all like to go to Cortina Di Ampezzo?'

"What's there?"

"Skiing!"

Cortina Di Ampezzo was more than we had expected. Snow covered mountains bathed in sunshine and balmy weather, this had been the site of the Winter Olympics in a previous year.

"It's hot," said Kurt, wiping his forehead as he searched for a parking spot.

"It's not hot, you're just not used to it," I replied. "Park over there just for now, then we'll find a hotel."

Cortina was full of hotels, it seemed like nothing but hotels, but even so we could find no accommodation, for everything was booked solid. We did find accommodation for one night, which would not give us time enough to ski, but as it was getting late and we were too tired to drive on we checked in and watched the other people ski, from our hotel window.

The next day we followed the road along the Gulf of Trieste, which reminded us of the Squamish highway. Trieste is an old city, beautifully situated. Doug and Laural thought Jugoslavia was looking rather neglected, but of course there are such spots in every country. We did not stop at Trieste, but continued on, noticing that the snow was beginning to melt. Of course, we excepted to find it again, in higher altitudes or back in Austria.

Just before we reached the Austrian border, we stopped for a bite to eat and noticed that Tito had joined us or rather, his picture had, for a huge portrait of him hung just over our table. Laural thought it might be nice to take a picture of all this. She was just reaching for her camera when a uniformed man came into the café. She almost dropped the camera in her haste to get it back into her bag. "I was sure he was going to arrest us," she whispered.

"Don't be silly, he's just here for lunch." Even so, he kept looking toward our table, which made Laural even more nervous and we eventually left to continue on towards Graz.

"You must be bored, always going to see our relatives," I said.

"Don't be silly, we enjoy it. We have never been here before, remember, and everything is interesting to us."

Graz came into sight, resting on its seven hills in the greenbelt of Austria.

Kurt's brother, Roland, had just built a new house but as not all the guest rooms were yet completed, had reserved rooms for Doug and Laural at a nearby inn. Kurt and I would stay at Roland's, and we assured Doug and Laural that if they couldn't understand the people at the inn or had any trouble, they should call us.

Roland's house was big, beautiful and brand new. The entrance hall was so huge a full orchestra could have played there and not crowded it. There was a fireplace in the middle to add to the coziness. As the other rooms of the house were of normal size, Kurt asked what the family did in that big hall.

"We entertain here. This you call a living room. You can even smoke here, Kurt."

"What do you mean, only here? I smoke anywhere!"

Kurt's brother was against smoking and Kurt abided by his wishes. At supper there were a few other guests in our honour and everyone tried their best English, including Roland. There was discussion as to our next stop, and Lech seemed to be the favourite. Laural suggested a vote, but as she and Doug would rather ski than do more sightseeing (for they had not done much skiing so far) we were off to Lech the next day, deciding to skip a few other stops instead.

I had never been there, nor had Kurt. It was really something else. There are really no words to describe it. All one could see was snow, snow to the left and snow to the right. No streets. No trees. No houses. Just snow all around us. "I've never seen anything like it," Doug said, and we all agreed. Had we collected all the snow in British Columbia in December it would not come close to this much. It was a skier's paradise!

We did eventually find the village, and another disappointment – no rooms. Now we blamed each other for not making reservations, parked the car and found a place to have a sandwich and watch the activity. We had thought that if we waited awhile there might be a cancellation at one of the hotels, but this turned out to be a vain hope. As the sun was setting, Doug suggested we move on to Vienna, for this would be no place to be stranded should it snow again – we'd never get out!

"Good thing Kurt is driving; I never knew Vienna is called *Wien*," said Doug.

"Nobody showed us around when we first arrived in Canada, and it was just as strange to us," I replied. "So how do you like Europe, apart from the signs?"

"I like it, but I wouldn't want to live here."

"Why not?"

Doug started to reply, hesitated, then said simply, "Because I love Canada."

"We love Canada, too, but you must admit Austria is beautiful – and the food – especially the food!" Kurt replied.

"Yes, what was that you ate the other day? Those black noodles...."

"*Rauchfangkehrer* Noodle – Chimneysweep Noodles," I translated.

"I would really like a good steak for a change," Doug said.

"And I would like Chinese food," I whispered. "There's supposed to be a good Chinese restaurant here in Vienna."

Kurt heard that. "You all must be crazy – wanting Chinese food in Vienna! That's like eating sauerkraut during a Canadian hockey game!"

We were still outside the city, and it seemed we were just going in circles. Nobody believed that Kurt had gone to university here at one time, since he couldn't find our way in to the city; but even though the city itself had not changed, the transportation system had. Once in the city, we tried to find the little hotel at which Fritz had made reservations for us. We decided to stop in a little café for a drink, and ask directions.

"The best way to find your hotel," they told us, "is to hire a taxi and follow it." We had no choice; we were tired and it was getting late, and we'd surely never find the hotel in the dark.

Over breakfast, Doug asked, "Don't you find it very expensive for an old hotel?" Here we go again.

"What's old in Canada is not the same here. This is historically old, which is different from an old hotel room in Hope or Penticton. Look out there, it's all history and all in walking distance – St. Stephan Cathedral, the famous Lipizaner Riding School, the Opera. What do you see when you look out a hotel room back home? Sure, it may be very modern, with a bathroom in every room, new beds. There are new hotel here too, and close to everything, but you pay a fortune. Now forget about crooked un-carpeted floors and let's go see the city."

We walked along Kaertnerstrasse, and did a little window-shopping. The prices are high, but you can get everything here. Laural suggested we take a bus tour as the walking was getting very tiring, and so we did.

The tour took us to famous cathedrals, to the graves of famous knights and kings. The guide was just explaining the location of the grave of

Maximilian in the basement of an old church when Doug leaned over and whispered, "How many Maximilians were there, anyway?"

"Why?" I whispered back.

"I remember when we were in Wiener Neustadt in the chapel of the Academy where Rommel had once lived, they also had a grave of a Maximilian."

I had to laugh, for I was confused too.

After the tour we tried to find a place to eat and while we were concentrating on that Doug was still trying to sort out the historical facts he had learned that day. "Remember," he said, "I took a picture of Baumkirchnerstrasse and then we went to the Academy. Don't you know?" he asked me.

"Yes, I know what you mean, but we were not allowed in the Academy.

My brother was there a few times, since he went to school with Rommel's son. Maybe he knows. We can ask him when we get back to Salzburg." Meanwhile, Kurt kept marching from one restaurant to the other, reading the menus posted in the windows. He was hungry for something special. Suddenly Laural spotted a red dragon sign and pulled me to one side. "What's over there?"

I looked and sure enough, it was a Chinese restaurant! Now Kurt noticed it too, and after a few objections agreed to try it. It was expensive, but it was the best Chinese food he had tasted.

We had one more day in Vienna, and then it was time to head back to Salzburg to pick up our things. Fritz had arranged a farewell dinner in Schloss Leopoldskron overlooking the castle with its gardens and ponds. We had lived there one summer long ago. My father had a job there when the castle was turned into a school for international students. They had come for lectures and for pleasures. Dad had been in charge of the staff. That had been such a long time ago. I remembered, as I ate my goulash now, so many things, and Fritz too kept asking "Do you remember this?" and "How can I forget that!"

And then it was time again to say goodbye, *Auf Wiedersehen*.

Chapter Nineteen

We Host The Media

Once back in the New World again, the trip quickly became memories and photographs (which I find myself reviewing over and over).

Midge was in hospital again, continuing her fight against cancer – but it was clear now that it was a losing battle.

For us, life was quickly resuming its usual routine, and as we prepared for another weekend trip to Whistler (for Kurt could hardly wait to go skiing) we received a piece of mail which would affect our plans for the next weeks.

The letter was from a friend of Kurt's brother Roland, who was planning to visit Canada to gather information for magazine articles for European publications. He asked if he could call on us and interview us for a series of articles on Austrian and German immigrants in Canada – how they live, work and play.

I showed Kurt the letter and he said, "Okay, he can come with us, as I have to go up north soon. Write him back quickly."

The week passed quickly as we caught up with the house and yard work that had piled up while we were away. Then the weekend, and another trip to Whistler! There was still snow on the mountains, and as we approached Garibaldi the landscape grew whiter and whiter.

"I hope they cleared the driveway at our cabin," I said to Kurt.

"I hope so. I told Swend to look after that before we left for Europe."

As we arrived at Edelweiss Village I noticed that curtains were open at most windows, so our friends were there; someone waved to us from Stan's window.

The driveway was indeed free of snow, but "The roof looks a little dangerous, don't you think?" I asked Kurt.

"No, we made a snow guard last year, remember? That helps quite a bit."

"All the same, park the car a little way from the house, just in cast."

"Don't worry so much, Agnes. Everything is under control." He has everything under control all the time. I thought I would like to be that way, unworried. Kurt keeps his worries inside, someone once said, and that is dangerous. It's much better if you don't keep it bottled up, because if it gets to be too much the bottle can explode. Much better to let your steam out all the time.

Stan was coming towards us through a tunnel of snow, his pipe in one hand while the other ruffled his curly hair in a familiar gesture. For the fist time, I noticed some grey in that hair.

"How are the world travelers?" he greeted us. We said we were fine and asked after Midge.

"She's not so good; she had a lot of pain and worst of all, her legs are so swollen she cannot ski anymore."

"Where is she now?"

"Here at the cabin."

"Why don't you both come over later, and see the pictures of our trip?"

Stan promised that they'd be over, and we went indoors.

The cabin was cold and damp, for no one had been there for some time. Vivian and Kurt Jr. were too busy with other things to make the trip to Whistler and of course, we had been away. Kurt went outside to fetch wood for the fire and noticed that someone had been helping himself to our pile. Evidently it had been pretty cold here, too.

With the fire leaping in the hearth the place came alive again, and it was quite cozy and warm by the time Midge and Stan arrived.

We sipped coffee and looked at the pictures, remembering little stories about the trip to tell them.

"Did you go to England, too?" Midge asked.

"Unfortunately, there was not enough time for that. We really spent very little time anywhere in order to cover all the territory."

"How was the skiing?" she wanted to know.

"We did not do much of that, either. We came pretty close, and went to some beautiful ski areas, but there was no accommodation. Did you ever hear of Lech Am Arlberg?" I asked them. "I have never seen so much snow in my entire life! No fooling. I was really turned on to ski. Imagine yourself in a desert of snow instead of sand. You could easily get snow-phobia."

"What is that?"

"Nothing. I just invented it."

A knock at he door heralded Roland and Vivian, with a plateful of Roland's special Danish pastries which we enjoyed with our coffee.

After a while we had enough of Europe and the men switched the conversation to politics while Midge, Vivian and I planned a *kaffeeklatsch* for the next day to which we'd invite all our lady friends while the men went skiing. As Midge couldn't ski now, I wanted to do something so she wouldn't miss it so much.

I planned to contribute the coffee and blueberry muffins, made from blueberries picked on Whistler last summer, and frozen. The size of the blueberries here is unbelievable, and Midge agreed. "I made jam last year," she said. "It didn't take long to pick enough for that. We had a few bucketfuls in no time and the jam turned out really well."

•••

The next day was a glorious spring day; the sun was shining, glinting off the snow that promised excellent skiing. As I tidied up from breakfast,

Alvin called to ask if she could drop by. "Of course," I said, and in a little while she arrived, wearing another gown. This one was a Hawaiian print, as they had just returned from a trip there. As she told me about the Islands, she said, "You really should go there, you and Kurt. Everyone should go there once in their lifetime. We've already booked for next year!"

"What do you think we should do about Midge?" she asked suddenly. "You know she had invited me over for coffee. Does one ignore her cancer, or talk about it?"

"I think Midge really wants to talk about it. She's a realist and she knows the score."

"Well, I'll bring some sherry," Alvin said as she lit a cigarillo and offered me one. "Who else is coming?"

"Well, everybody who will not go skiing. Stan said we should all go over again in the evening."

"Isn't that too much for Midge?" she asked.

"I think he prefers to have everybody come there, since it is difficult for Midge to get around now."

Midge greeted us with a big smile and seemed very cheerful. We sat down at the bar. Each of the condominiums is the same size as its neighbours, but each has its own style. This was very West Coast: everything was made of driftwood – all the furniture, the table which is a masterpiece, the lamps, the chairs and the bar. The bar is one solid curved piece of wood which Stan found in the Queen Charlotte Islands and brought back by plane with some difficulty.

Midge's trademark forsythias were in the window, and mixed in with the bouquet were some pussy willows which she said they had found along the Squamish highway.

"There are plenty, but these ones are especially beautiful. "Stan picked them for me," she explained, gazing at the flowers. "Stan will get you some; just ask him. And you can invite him for coffee – he always likes your coffee."

"It must be good skiing today," Vivian said. "I know the men will be

hungry – we'd better leave them some of your delicious blueberry muffins."

"I've got some more – don't worry," I said. "And here come Ruth, so
the men will not be far behind."

"Are you kidding? They always have to have the last run. What time is
it now?"

"It's already five o'clock!"

"In that case if they aren't on their way, they're in the L'Apres."

Ruth looked all sun and wind-burned; the sun is picking up strength
at this time of year. Some distance behind her, we could see the men coming, tanned and sport looking. Kurt was wearing his Austrian checkered
shirt – the newest thing here – and had his jacket tied round his waist, like
the other men.

"It must be warm up there. I really should go skiing tomorrow. How
about it, Ruth? You pick me up in the morning," I said to her.

In two and threes they came straggling in, to form our happy Whistler
family group. The women went home and brought their suppers back to
Stan and Midge's and the men collected beer and wine: no restaurant
could have competed with the spread.

After everyone had eaten they sat back to talk about their day on the
mountain. I watched Midge gazing longingly out the window at the
mountain beyond as the men kept raving about how fabulous the snow
was. Alvin tried to switch the subject away from skiing. Engrossed in their
conversation, the skiers did not understand what she was trying to do,
and one even said "Just because you don't ski doesn't mean we should all
talk about something else!"

But Stan saw and came to the rescue, commenting on the new development, and more general things. But old habits die hard and someone
was soon asking for music for dancing. "Shall I go get my record player?"
my neighbour was asking. I kicked him in the leg and whispered, "no
dancing today, not here. Midge isn't up to it."

I suggested we talk about our trip; Alvin and Swend were to tell us
about Hawaii and we would recount our adventures in Europe. So we

went from warm tropical winds to cold Alpine snows as we listened to the other couple's adventures, Kurt suddenly looked at me and said, "You know, I think we should go to Hawaii next." I was quite agreeable.

•••

I had been studying a bit about the history and geography of our area in preparation for our visitor from overseas, for if he was going to write an article he'd probably be asking a lot of questions and I wanted to give him right answers.

He arrived in due course and we found him to be a very pleasant young man, eager to learn anything and everything. His English was excellent, which surprised and delighted Vivian and Kurt Jr.

As we ate dinner, I saw that he was making a note of everything we told him. "I hope you don't write that I burned the steaks," I joked. "We'll have to check your articles before you leave!"

The following day we drove him through Stanley Park, and he was full of questions, wanting to know how old and how tall the trees were. This was something neither Kurt nor I had studied up on, so I quickly interjected, "Did you know we had a typhoon here in 1962 and many of the trees were blown down and destroyed?"

Kurt looked at me in astonishment. "You were away at the time on a business trip," I reminded him.

"Oh, *Ja*, I remember it was called Typhoon Frieda. I'd really like to know why they all have female names. Have you ever heard of a hurricane called Kurt?" he asked.

We parked the car and walked through the grounds, visiting the aquarium where we didn't have to answer any questions – we picked up a pamphlet and handed it to our guest. After a tour of the marine life we walked around the zoo area, which I always enjoyed – especially the monkeys.

We lunched at the Café Heidelberg on Robsonstrasse. Our guest wanted to walk around the city, but we advised him that while we could walk up and down Robsonstrasse and around the downtown core, one really needed a car to get around Vancouver and see everything. "It's not like Europe," we reminded him.

"What is the population of Vancouver?" was his next question.

"It hit a million in 1962 in the Greater Vancouver area but what is now I couldn't say. I know they had a big fire in 1886, you can write about that." I just had to say what I had recently learned. But Kurt just smiled and said, "Don't trust her; sometimes she gets the figures mixed up."

Kurt had taken the day off so we could drive out to Whistler and spend the night there, but it was a disappointment.

The weather did not cooperate; it was so foggy on the highway that one could almost cut it, and near Britannia the smell was horrible. Our friend rolled his car window down to attempt to get rid of the odour, but that just made it worse.

"It's from the pulp mill at Woodfibre," we told him. "Don't write about this. Wait until tomorrow; you'll see, it will be quite different." We did stop at Britannia so he could photograph the old mine, but we were not sure how the pictures would turn out, considering the thickness of the fog.

Hans loved our Alpenhaus, as he called it, and after turning on the heat to have the place cozy for our return, we drove him around to see the rest of the area, and Alta Lake. There were many more new houses which we had not seen, and building was going on everywhere. The names were almost impossible to translate into German, as we couldn't even understand them in English!

We stopped at Rudi's for one of his fabulous steaks; business was slow as the ski season was over, so Rudi had time to make us a *Kaiserschmarn* for dessert.

"I think I have plenty to write about," said Hans. "I'd like to write about you, Kurt."

"About me?" Kurt said, surprised.

"I find it all fascinating, how you made it all, lost it all and started again. You don't mind?"

"No, I don't mind, if you can't find anything better. But wait until we got to Prince George – there is a lot of history along the way. And Prince

George itself is interesting. Did you know they ski in summer up there, on sand, and play golf in the winter in the snow?"

After spending the night in Whistler we hoped for better weather for the return journey, but it was still quite foggy, and as we drew nearer to Vancouver it started to rain. You can always be sure of rain.

It was still raining as we passed through Vancouver and continued to the Fraser Valley, clearing up just as we came close to Hope. Hans was busily snapping away with his camera and scribbling with his pencil as we drove. I was glad he didn't hesitate to ask us to stop here and there, for when Kurt and I drive the only time we stop is if we need gas, or to go the bathroom.

In Yale, we visited the oldest church in British Columbia, built in 1859 when the miners had flocked here during the Klondike gold rush.

Hans and I were busily reading the pamphlets we had picked up along the way. "Did you know, Kurt, that Ashcroft was the copper capital of the world?"

He gestured with his cigarettes toward the nearby river. "That's the Fraser River," he informed us, "just in case you don't know."

"Oh, *ja*. Clever. Very clever."

I asked if we could go to Barkerville.

"What do you want there again? We've been there so many times. You know, Hans, if I were to take Agnes along on my business trips as a rule I would never get any business done. She likes to run around in ghost towns and out of the way places."

"It would take almost a lifetime to see it all," Hans replied. "It's so big! You see that sign, 'The World's Biggest Hamburger'? We should go and have one."

"I don't like hamburgers," Kurt said.

"I'm sure they have something else," I replied. "We should stop there. I always wanted to and you never would."

The world's biggest hamburger was not all that good and was too much. We couldn't eat it all. We ate what we could and then drove on.

In Quesnel, we examined a site for a proposed school. Kurt would be bidding on the job. We saw a sign advertising a *Gasthaus* and I wanted to stop for a coffee or beer there.

"We just had something and here you want to stop again. Let's drive on to Prince George. On the way back, maybe."

"Aren't we going to Barkerville?" I asked.

"I don't think it's open," Kurt said.

"Let's try anyway." And Kurt obediently turned in the direction of Bakerville.

It was late evening when we arrived, and the sun was setting on the old barns and wagons scattered along the roadside. It was peaceful and quiet; the place looked deserted. As we drove along we explained to Hans that this was once a lively place when they first discovered "gold in them thar hills."

"I thought it was a place where they make westerns," he replied.

"Once a year they do something like that. During the summer they recreate the past and breathe life into those old wooden buildings."

Now, empty, it was as I said, "spooky."

"Anybody home?" I yelled into the empty houses. Suddenly I heard voices. "Do you hear anything?" I asked the other two.

"It's just the wind playing with the old doors. They don't look so solid anymore," Kurt said. "Let's go."

"No, I want to have a look in there. Come along. I don't want to look alone."

"First she wants to go to Barkerville and then she is scared of the wind," he joked to Hans.

I was glad Hans was curious and brave enough to push open that door. Behind the door were a few young people in their teens, high on something. We had seen no cars or other vehicles and wondered how they had gotten there. They looked as frightened to see us in the doorway, as we were to see them in the abandoned town. "Leave us alone. Go away," said the leader of the group, and we did just that.

I later read what Hans had written about the episode: *In Barkerville, a ghost town in northern British Columbia, we came across a*

few lost flower children hanging around in an old barn – maybe waiting for a
better world, and thought they could find it in their trips to Fantasyland. These
kids travel far and high, but the higher they go, the farther they fall.

"That's being kind," I said to Hans.

"Yes, I feel sorry for them rather than angry. We have a new breed in Germany: they have short hair, some actually shaved heads – blood painted all over their body – the Punks, they call themselves. Another product of the times. They are not gentle like the flower children. Flower children want peace; the Punks want war."

"Pretty scary?"

"It is indeed."

"Remember the Schlurfs?" Kurt asked. "No, I guess not, you were too young, or maybe not even born. They used to comb their hair back and used a lot of grease to hold it in place. I guess they got their inspiration from Al Capone and the gangster types. Maybe another product of the times."

While we were having dinner, Hans kept asking all kinds of questions and with the help of the restaurant owner, the waitress and a few guests we learned some facts about Barkerville. The waitress produced a paper placemat that detailed the whole story of the town. We learned that Barkerville had been the Gold Capital of the Cariboo in its heyday during the 1860's, and is now a sixty-five acre historic park. There were stories of those who had made it and lost it in the Klondike, among them Billy Barker for whom the town was named. The placemat also mentioned the Theatre Royal, which we were familiar with because our daughter Vivian played a saloon girl there each summer during the recreation of those hectic frontier times.

• • •

It is always interesting what one learns when one has a visitor from another country. Everyone in the restaurant was taking an interest in Hans and wanted to tell him their story, particularly one old miner who would not shut-up. Kurt bought him a half-dozen beers and the garrulous old boy seemed to be a fountain of information about everything!

Finally we left to find a bed for the night at the Inn of the North. In the bar for a nightcap, we found a crowd of people celebrating the winners of a downhill skiing competition.

"I told you before, Hans. Austria is the father of downhill skiing in the snow, but Prince George invented skiing in the sand."

"Doesn't it ruin their skis?" Hans asked.

"I guess so, but they usually use beat-up skis, I understand. You should try it once, Kurt," I said. "He is crazy about skiing, Hans. You should see him in winter. Every weekend we go to our sanctuary on Whistler. He is unhappy the whole week if he misses a weekend."

Hans interrupted me with a tug on my arm. "Who are those strange-looking people who just peeked in the door?" he asked.

"Oh, those are Hutterites. They are a strict religious sect, like the Mennonites; they run farm communities and stay apart from the world, wearing turn-of-the-century clothes.

"There is nothing un-modern about the farm equipment or techniques, though. They have all the latest and run very successful, profitable farms, they say. I'd tell you more, but I'm too tired." I bid them goodnight and left them in the bar. It was some time later when I awoke to hear Hans and Kurt singing some German lullaby on their way to their rooms. I hoped they wouldn't waken the whole house; and while I was happy that Kurt was feeling so well these days, wished he'd take it easy with the beer sometimes!

The next day we were on the road again for Grande Prairie.

"Look at the scenery – wild roses along the roadside – what are those beautiful red flowers?" Hans cried.

"That's Indian paintbrush, Hans. And the wild rose is the provincial flower of Alberta, just as the dogwood is for BC. I hope you have a colour film. I just think it's beautiful here!"

Kurt laughed at this and said, "Agnes want to move up here when we retire."

"And will you do it?" Hans asked.

"No way. I retire on Whistler," Kurt replied quickly.

"You are building up here. Isn't it pretty far from Vancouver?"

"Yes. We usually fly but you wouldn't see much that way. But for business, you couldn't drive all the time," Kurt said.

"How is business up here?"

"Much better than in British Columbia right now," Kurt answered. "They have black gold up here. It we have time, we'll take you to Leduc where the big oil strike was first made in February 1947. That first well spewed oil for almost six months before it caught fire."

It was still light when we arrived at Grande Prairie, and we arrived at our rented house to find it empty; Kurt Jr. was at the job site. We let ourselves in with our key, made some coffee and opened a beer for Hans and Kurt. Then we all left to see the job site, where everyone was still at work at full speed. While Kurt inspected the project, Hans and I walked around town – quickly done as there was only one main street, beyond which are golden fields and blue skies.

Kurt arrived with the foreman and Kurt Jr. in tow and we all went to get something to eat and afterward found accommodation for Hans, as there was not enough room at the house for us all.

We decided that Hans and I would go sightseeing to Edmonton the next day, while Kurt handled a few things in Grande Prairie, and then we'd start back for Vancouver.

"Too bad you're too early for Klondike Days," Kurt Jr. said. "That would really have been interesting but there's still a lot to see."

Our trip to Edmonton was a disaster; we hit a storm and the wind was terrible. We had to cut our visit short if we didn't want to get stuck in the mud on the highway. Still, it was an interesting visit – everything is interesting the first time!

We returned to Vancouver by way of Prince George and called on Ushi and Erhardt but, as we had not phoned to let them know we were coming, we missed them – they weren't home.

Back in Vancouver, Hans thanked us for taking him on what he called "this most interesting trip of my life."

We were just unpacking when the phone rang, and Kurt answered it.

It was a skiing buddy of Kurt's saying "Sorry about your friend."

"What happened?" I heard Kurt say, and then "What? She died?"

Immediately I thought that Midge had finally succumbed to the cancer, but no, to my astonishment Kurt said that it was Alvin that had passed away.

"Alvin?" We just had coffee together on Whistler not too long ago! There was nothing wrong with Alvin! How? Why?"

We did not wait too long for the answers to those questions, for our daughter Vivian phoned and told us that Alvin had died of a stroke.

"Alvin was our neighbour in Whistler, nice to know, nice to talk to. Hans, you go and help yourself to anything you can find. Kurt and I must go and see her family now."

The family was in shock and there was not much we could do or say, but we hoped our presence gave some comfort. Her dog was wandering from room to room searching for her and I noticed Alvin's Hawaiian gown hanging in a corner of her room – the same one she had been wearing the last time I saw her. I couldn't believe she was gone, or understand why she was taken now.

It was late when we returned home, and Hans was already in bed.

"He has only a few more days before he leaves," I reminded Kurt.

The weather had remained clear and the fruit trees and roses were all in bloom so I thought it might be a good idea to invite a few friends for the weekend in honour of our guest.

"Sure, why not? We can go to Whistler another weekend."

I sensed that Kurt really didn't want to go to Whistler just now.

While he was at the office one day, I took Hans to Grouse Nest, the restaurant atop Grouse Mountain. "We used to ski here all the time. Whistler didn't exist for us then," I said. "This gondola we are riding in was built in 1966; before that we had to take a chair up."

We had a good table at the window, and the view was terrific, clear of clouds and fog. The lunch, too, was very good, and afterward we walked around a little. I showed him The Cut, the run where I had learned to ski.

Our farewell party was quite a success; everyone was there except our dear friends, Alvin and Swend. We talked a great deal about them, about Whistler, and our lives in Canada. As most of our friends had originally come from Europe Hans picked up a wealth of information for all the articles he could wish.

Chapter Twenty

A Sanctuary in the Mountains

Our visitor had returned to Europe, and Kurt and I took advantage of the summer weather to drive up to Whistler and touch up the cabin's paintwork. It was so peaceful – so many were enjoying summer activities or holidays away from the ski slopes. It was not quiet further down the road, as we saw when we drove to the store for more paint. There was feverish activity going on in the village and on Blackcomb; we heard that an Aspen, Colorado company had put some money in to the project to have it ready for winter of 1982. I wished that could have happened with Brohmridge, but it seemed that this development was fated to remain a dream.

"Blackcomb will be nice when it is all finished," Kurt said, "but for my skiing, I am quite happy with Whistler. Besides, it's closer to our house; we just have to walk there."

"I'm sure they'll have more transportation later on," I replied.

"Actually," he said, "what they should have done is develop Brohmridge, Powder Mountain and Blackcomb; they would have a ski terrain unequalled in the world! Well, maybe not the world – but certainly in North America."

"It's amazing how skiing has taken over. I remember when we first went to Grouse, hardly anybody was up there skiing. You could not even buy skis or an outfit. I remember only one ski shop, The Two Skiers, and now ski shops are mushrooming all over the place."

We stood back to admire our paintwork, which had to dry before we could put on the next coat. "It looks pretty good," I said, "and the flowers in the window boxes look much better, too."

We sat there, the two of us, looking up at Whistler and enjoying the long summer day which seemed to linger on. We felt good just being alive, just the two of us, happy to still have one another....

In the morning a neighbour dropped by with the bad news that Midge was in hospital again. Why is it, I wondered, that always after a nice day a very bad one follows; and after a very good time, comes a very bad one?

On Sunday we drove back to Vancouver and I enjoyed, as always, the lovely scenery along the highway. The ocean was calm and scattered with fishing boats and sailboats. A train was roaring beside us and the snow-capped mountains formed a backdrop for it all. Circling above, completing the picture, was a rare bald eagle. I marveled again, as I had hundreds of times before, at the beauty of the country.

Kurt never seemed to see the passing scene; his concentration was centered on the road ahead. He never trusted me to drive, and I had no desire to take the wheel on that stretch of road.

Vivian came over for dinner that evening and we decided to order Chinese food. Kurt didn't mind it once in a while. The doctor had advised him to stay away from fatty foods, and this made a good excuse for ordering my favourite Chinese food.

After dinner we all went to the hospital to visit Midge. She smiled as always, but we saw it caused her pain. For Midge, now, the situation was hopeless, and we were helpless except to sit there and watch her suffering. She was surrounded by flowers, including a bunch of her trademark forsythia, probably from her own garden. Stan sat holding her hand, and their daughter sat at her other side. We talked about our trip to the Prairies, Kurt's job in Alberta, our visitor from overseas, and avoided mentioning Whistler, knowing how she must miss it. But she asked anyway, "How is Whistler" She was hungry for news of the mountain she loved.

"They are working on the new mountain now," said Kurt, "and the village is coming along fine."

"What about Brohmridge?" she asked with concern.

"I guess I can write that one off," replied Kurt. We all remembered the collapse of the project, and how Kurt had not been himself for so long after.

The nurse came in at this point and gently reminded us it was time to leave, and as we moved toward the door we promised to return and visit soon. We asked Stan to come by the house on the way home to have a drink with us.

Stan was in a terrible state when he arrived, and we had a terrible time calming him down. He downed one cognac after another, and than sat, the pipe cold in his mouth, his voice filled with emotion as he talked of Midge. As I made coffee, I said, "You never know, Stan. It is possible they could invent a new drug for cancer treatment any day."

"I am sure of it," he said, "but it will be too late for Midge." We all knew that, but were reluctant to say it. We sat awkwardly and were relieved when Swend showed up. Had Kurt phoned him? The atmosphere eased with his arrival.

• • •

Summer came to an end and the skiers started waxing their skis, preparing for the snow which would soon be falling for those who could still enjoy life and good health. Once again, they will be heading for the hills, those kings and queens of the mountains. Last time we were all together, I noticed more grey hairs and some deeper lines, but most of our friends were still in good shape. Actually, I liked Kurt's grey hair; funny that men seem to look better, more distinguished with grey hair. One never thinks that of women.

"We can still out ski all the young people," they would say, "and we'll ski until we die!" For the lovers of such a sport, this was as important to their existence as breathing. They couldn't live without it.

•••

It was a watercolour blue sky and lots of snow when I went up to Whistler with Kurt one Sunday. There were not too many people and not too many moguls. I liked skiing with Kurt, especially when I don't fall too often. I was in great shape that day, and thought, "I can really ski; when it's just the two of us!" I knew it would not last, for soon everybody would be on the slopes and the mountain would be crowded – but for the moment, I enjoyed the empty runs. We went down the Olympic Run, which was just perfect – no ice – I wished it could be like that all the time. At the base we met some friends and decided to take the shuttle bus back to Whistler Village and lunch at L'Apres. It had certainly changed from the days when we had danced polkas there. The old band is gone, replaced by a disco, but I can still hear them playing *Heilige Berge* (Holy Mountain) as I sit in the familiar surroundings.

Life changes, I thought. We change. No, actually, life itself does not seem to change; rather we are the ones who change life; it's like a giant computer, its output depending on what each programmer feeds into it. The seasons continue, the rain, the snow and the sun take their turns on the earth. There is nothing that can be done to change that, and so people change the sounds and sights. The music Kurt and I enjoyed is now called old-fashioned, and music of today will soon be called the same. Everything seems to be moving so much faster now; life itself is lived at a faster pace. Where are the days, my friend? Still there – a little scarcer, a little shorter and quite a bit faster. Now when our friends gather, there is less talk of fun and games and more discussion about retirement. Everybody has a different plan, a different place. Some even want to go home to the old country, but Kurt is persistent. He retires on Whistler, and soon. I said, as I had so many times before, "But there is no doctor or hospital on Whistler. It will not work."

One of our friends suggested, "Why don't you retire to Squamish? Then you're right between Vancouver and Whistler." He was joking, but we considered it seriously.

On the way home I suggested we stop and look around the new area they called Garibaldi. It was a little community outside Squamish we had never really noticed until the highway was rebuilt and rerouted past it. There was a small shopping center and a golf course, and we had heard there were some beautiful homes in the area called Garibaldi Highlands.

As Kurt tired more easily from skiing, he was agreeable to leave early and so we headed south to Garibaldi. The whole area was unbelievable. The golf course, surrounded by mountains, was beautiful by itself, but the homes! Many of them rivaled the luxury dwellings in the British Properties, and the whole area featured underground wiring so there was an unobstructed view of the mountains. It was like Switzerland! We came to the street known only as The Boulevard, with its wide grassy median and Mount Garibaldi in the background, and thought we could easily be in Austria again. I thought to myself, if Kurt could get used to the idea this would be a perfect place to retire. He would have his mountains forever at his doorstep and we could go to Vancouver anytime.

"What do you think?" I asked. "Isn't it beautiful here?"

"We will see," was all Kurt would say as he made his way down to the highway to drive to Vancouver.

The more I thought about the move the better I liked it, and I had a feeling Kurt did too when he said, "When I have time, we'll go and look for something and put our house on the market. I want to retire soon, anyway. We can rent the house out in the meantime." It seemed everything was solved. How simple it seemed, and how happy I was that for once we both agreed on something and were actually looking forward to our retirement years.

I expected we would spend Christmas at Whistler again this year, though it appeared we would not be able to stay afterward. Both Kurts (Sr. and Jr.) were at Grande Prairie and very busy; they would have to return to the jobsite right after the holiday and not be able to stay over

New Year's. I decided to have a small tree in Vancouver and plan on going out to Whistler after, for a day or two of skiing before Kurt had to return to Grande Prairie. It was thirty-six below there and I decided warm clothes would be appropriate gifts!

•••

The Christmas tree was up (not such a small one after all) and decorated. As Vivian was busy and the men were away, I did the job myself, all in red, and was very proud of my efforts as it did look fine. Of course, I tried to dramatize to the family what a difficult time I had had bringing the tree home and setting it up, but my son scoffed that he had heard that I had bought the tree from Boy Scouts, who had brought it right to the house for me. It was set up according to custom in the Glass Room, as we called the room with the glass skylight, and there with the fireplace lit and the candles on the tree reflected in the glass above we gathered again. This was a room for special occasions, and at Christmas it was my favourite room of the house. This Christmas Eve we had Kurt Jr. and Vivian staying over with us as they still had no families of their own and once again we had our children waiting for Santa Claus with us.

Santa was good to us and made us very happy. Christmas morning we took several hours as usual to unwrap everything and joke together over old times.

"Remember, Vivian, the hope chest?"

"Oh, yes. Daddy made a hope chest for me and put all my presents in it. I thought all I got was a wooden box! I still treasure that chest; I will always keep it."

"Where do you have it now?"

"At my place, with my TV on it. Oh, look what I got! A book: *The Skier's Bible*. Is that a hint?" We all laughed.

•••

On the way to Whistler the mountains and trees seemed more beautiful than ever; it was as though someone had dusted icing sugar over all. The sun glistened through the branches, and a black raven sat starkly silhouetted against the cloudless blue sky. Somewhere out of sight an airplane droned, breaking the silence. With the decorated houses completing the picture, we had a true winter wonderland.

"It should be good skiing," Kurt said. We all agreed.

"Maybe we can all go skiing together. I can show you what I learned form Dad, and with my new boots, it should be interesting," I said. "Actually I was going to keep my old leather boots but Dad insists I will ski better."

"It's just like driving an old model car. You can't go that fast," he says.

"I don't want to go faster anyway. I guess nobody is wearing leather boots any more. They've become antique. I should keep them."

"Sure. You're an antique too!" replied Kurt.

We thought Swend had arrived after all, for half the duplex was lit up and the big tree outside was decorated, its lights on; but no, it was not Swend, just some friends of his. All was in darkness at Stan's, the curtains drawn and the familiar forsythias missing this year from the window.

•••

We went skiing together the next day; at least, we went up the chair together, but then each went in different directions as everyone found old friends. Kurt met up with Leo and I skied with Ruth. She invited us over for drinks that evening, and when we arrived we saw Mark, Branko. Szenka – almost the whole gang. Almost.

We talked, played music, danced a little, but as Branko said, it was not the same anymore. "I used to know everybody on the mountain. Now I don't meet anybody all day long. Either the mountain is getting bigger or our circle is getting smaller. Where is everybody skiing these days?" he asked.

"Well, there are new runs. You could not miss people when there was only one run, but now it's getting bigger and more and more people are skiing. The times are gone when we had the mountain practically to ourselves."

"I guess so," Branko agreed, as he poured some more of his home-made wine.

Afterward, we walked home through the snow and paused to glance at the still-dark windows next door. The car was gone, so the children must be out somewhere. The fire was out and it was cold, so I turned on the heat while Kurt fetched himself a beer. There was a note on the table, which we figured was from Vivian or Kurt Jr. telling us when to expect them.

"Stan phoned," it read. "Midge has died." That was all.

I kept reading it over and over again. "What day is it?" I asked. December 27, 1979. "I wonder if she died today or yesterday?"

"What difference does it make?" asked Kurt.

"No difference. No difference at all."

The darkness next door seemed to be in the room with me. I suddenly shivered.

"Do you realize, Kurt, within a short time we lost both neighbours."

"I know," he said sadly. He had liked Midge so much; a fine woman, a lovely person, our friend.

The next morning, the message was passed on to our friends and I thought that Branko had been right, that it was not the same anymore. Our circle was getting smaller. Midge had always wished to be buried on Whistler, her ashes scattered on the slopes of the Holy Mountain. We supposed that Stan would fulfill her last wish.

We all talked about that and thought it would be nice if we all went with Stan on her last run, if he wanted it that way. In the meantime, there was the funeral service to find out about. The family had requested no flowers, but I had to take a bunch of forsythias – I was determined to get some from somewhere and force them to bloom one last time for our friend, Midge.

And so we buried another friend.

We all went to the church service, but on the mountain Stan wanted to be alone when he said goodbye, finally, to his wife. Somewhere high on Whistler the snow turned grey for a brief moment until some new snowflakes fell gently to cover it all with a white blanket. Midge is with Helmut now, and near us forever.

•••

It was very quiet now in Edelweiss Village. All the action was down where they were building the new Town Centre, or over at the new Blackcomb development. The mountain keeps growing but our circle gets smaller. I had less desire to go to Whistler now, for I was afraid I'd meet Stan or Swend and not know what to say to them.

"Let's go to Mount Hood for a change of scenery," I suggested. "Our place on Whistler is like a ghost town. The Americans don't come up that often, maybe because the gasoline prices have gone up and everything in Canada is so expensive now."

Kurt agreed that Mound Hood sounded like a good idea, and we decided that if the children didn't intend to use the Whistler place, we'd rent it out.

I looked forward to the trip, wanting to stop here and there, and especially at Portland to shop at the huge shopping plazas. Kurt drove fast as usual, making good time, but I had to pull his sleeve if I wanted to stop. "You should go and race," I said. "This highway has a speed limit, remember."

"*Ja, ja*," he laughed. "Don't worry. I won't get you killed."

"Where are we staying? Did you make reservations?"

"*Ja*, in Portland somewhere. I can't remember; look in my jacket, the slip should be there."

At this point, I glanced at Kurt and saw he looked unwell.

"What is the matter?" I demanded.

"Oh, nothing."

But I knew there was something and eventually he admitted he was having chest pains.

"Turn around!" I screamed. "Let's go to the hospital!"

"No, I'm okay."

"Turn around, please. If you don't want to go to a doctor or a hospital let's drive home. I am not going to Mount Hood."

"You are the one who wanted to go!"

"I know," I said. "But not when you have pains. TURN AROUND!" I yelled so loud that Kurt did turn around, and stopped for a while to rest – then on we drove back to Vancouver.

I counted every mile.

"My God! Vancouver seems so far away," I thought. "We'll never be there!"

But there was the sign, and I really enjoyed, for once, all the rain for it meant we were really home.

After a few days' rest, Kurt felt all right again, but the following weekend we went to buy a house. Kurt seemed to have realized that if he did not retire soon it would be too late; and business was not too good, anyway.

We decided to put our Whistler retreat on the market – a tough decision, but if we bought a house in Garibaldi we wouldn't need the cabin. It was getting too expensive to keep up all of our properties! So we had a lot of work ahead of us, packing up things which had accumulated in two houses over twenty-five years. Now if only we could find a really nice house; that would make the move easier.

The saleswoman drove us all around Garibaldi and we saw many lovely homes – and then suddenly, there it was. We both knew it was our home as soon as we saw it from the outside: cedar and glass, beautiful and new. It had many similarities to our old house and we both fell in love with it. It is so seldom that we agree immediately but in this case, we were both sure this was the house for us. We bargained back and forth and when we finally agreed on a price we were delighted.

It was close to Easter and Kurt wanted to go up to Whistler. "Go alone," I told him. "I am too busy packing here." So Kurt went, but was back the same day and that evening we made the now-familiar trip to the hospital. Another attack.

Why was this happening to us? Why to Kurt? Was it because he was in the war – because he worked too hard – because he smokes too much? There were so many others who fit that description and yet they were spared. I was glad that all the packing kept me too busy to worry, as I usually did. But I hoped that the house would soon sell so that we could have peace and move to our new home in the mountains.

I felt time was running out. The doctor had told me this last attack was a bad one, and that if Kurt didn't retire he would not have much chance of a full recovery.

"But he is retiring, doctor. We just bought our retirement house. Oh, please help him; please help him to get well!" He reassured me they were doing all they could, and as I hung the phone I noticed that it was just 8:30 a.m. – I could have breakfast knowing that for now, Kurt was all right. I had just put coffee on when I felt the house shake slightly: not too hard, but enough to worry me. Was it the furnace? No, that was all right. I checked over the whole house but everything was in order, so I went on with my breakfast and soon forgot the incident. I put the radio on for company and very shortly thereafter the music was interrupted by an announcement which solved the mystery of the shaking house. "At 8:32 a.m. Mount St. Helens erupted in the largest explosion of this century on the North American continent."

Throughout the morning there were announcements and discussions of the eruption and when they mentioned Mount Hood, I really listened. I had not known that Mount Hood, too, was a volcanic mountain. I dug out the pamphlet we had saved from a trip to Oregon and found it, complete with photos of Mount Hood and Mount St. Helens in all its winter splendor. What a name for an angry mountain! So the mountains were not as peaceful as they looked and it seemed they could be quite deadly. The newscaster was saying that the last eruption had been one hundred and twenty-three years ago when I decided I had heard enough, and turned off the radio.

I made a point of visiting Kurt twice a day for a short period, watching his beating heart on the monitor. There were other visitors there when I arrived this day, and he was in good spirits and no pain. His heart seemed to have stabilized again and he was already talking about coming home. But the doctor was in no hurry to release him because he knew the minute Kurt left the hospital so he would resume his life at full speed – which was one reason why he never recovers completely and had had so many relapses.

Vivian came down from Barkerville and Kurt Jr. came home from Alberta and although Kurt said it was unnecessary for them to have done so, he was very pleased to see them. He told Vivian to make reservations for all of us to go to Hawaii. I was as astonished as the children at Kurt's insistence. "All of us?" Vivian asked.

"All of us." No one dared argue with him, not with the heart monitor going above his head, so we just agreed to everything, meanwhile thinking – "Is he joking?" He isn't even out of the hospital and plans to go to Hawaii. And we have the house on the market and packing to do...."

On the way out, Vivian asked me, "Mum, what shall we do?"

"Make reservations for Hawaii," I said.

"Maybe we should ask the doctor first," Kurt Jr. suggested, to which we all agreed.

"Why not?" The doctor said when we asked him. "Once he is out, he'll be better off in Hawaii than on the ski slopes."

"But the heat?" I said.

"Just take it easy."

Suddenly I was looking forward to going to Hawaii. Perhaps not everyone makes reservations to go there while still in hospital, but with Kurt everything is possible. He was always very sure of himself, always knowing what to do in every situation. I hoped he was right, now, but we couldn't have convinced him otherwise anyway so we may as well agree and go.

"Hawaii!" Alvin had once said. "Every person should go there once in their life."

●●●

Once Kurt was out of the hospital he set about dissolving his business, while I continued dissolving the households. On the weekend it was off to Whistler once more – but the sight of boxes piled everywhere hardly pleased us. Stan came over, but his repeated mumbling that an era was gone didn't help our mood much, and when Hans dropped by and asked, "Where did the *Gemutlichkeit* go?" It was too much for me. I went outside so nobody could see my tears, which flowed freely down into the trough. No, moving is not easy.

Cars were passing by on the highway, and occasionally one would honk a greeting – maybe friends or just happy tourists; they were all headed for the new village, anyway. Big things were planned there – the Shell Cup, the Molson Cup, The World Cup races, and just plain skiing for a lot of people.

I went into the house again to make some coffee. "If I can't find the dishes, we'll have to drink it out of the paper cups," I said.

"I think we will manage." Maybe, since we're all together, we should go to Rudi's for dinner." Everyone agreed to this but once at this favourite restaurant we saw it too had changed. Now it was not skiers one found at Rudi's, but construction workers. They were trying to get the buildings under roof before the snow fell. The inside work can be finished all year round, but one never knows when the snow will fall here; it may come early or not at all but in any case, one has to plan for it.

It was certainly not the usual weekend in Whistler.

We stopped at Garibaldi on our way back to the city, to look at our new house again. The more we looked the more we liked it. We sat on the steps outside the empty house and made plans that helped us forget the melancholy of leaving our homes in Whistler and West Vancouver.

"I will have my workshop downstairs, and we will make a *Bauerstube* downstairs, something like a pub but more in an alpine style. It will give me something to do while you go shopping in Vancouver," Kurt joked. "And if I want to go skiing it's no big deal, we are so close."

From the living room we could see the mountains, and that was all that mattered – we were back in the mountain forever. I remember when we began our refugee march so long ago and we followed the flat, open road I asked my father, "Where are we going?"

"To the mountains. We'll be safe, there," he replied.

We walked around the house, inside and out, until the sun set behind the Holy Mountains.

"Let's keep this a secret from our friends," I said. "They'll never guess where we bought our house."

"How long do you think you can keep a secret?" Kurt replied, and with that we drove away.

•••

Winter 1980. As the snow fell in Vancouver we were preparing to go to Hawaii. It was not easy to find our suitcase and warm-weather things, since the house was all in boxes. It was sold just a week before our departure, which meant we'd be moving to our new retirement home just as soon as we returned from our trip. Everyone was glad of the chance to get away from having to face our feeling at moving. The memories of twenty-five years haunted us as we moved from room to room; this was not just another house, it had been our home. I shivered.

"It's cold in here," I said to Kurt. "Let's make a fire."

"Pretty soon you'll say it's too hot. You'll be warm soon enough in Hawaii – it can get up to one hundred degrees Fahrenheit there, you know."

I wondered if that was a healthy climate for a person with a heart trouble, but kept my thoughts to myself. Kurt had made up his mind long ago to live his life as he pleased, even if it meant cutting it short.

As I found and packed my flight bag I realized I wouldn't need to take as much as if we were going to Europe; and always, in the back of my mind, was Alvin saying, "Everyone should go to Hawaii once in their lifetime."

•••

While others prepared for Christmas or headed for Whistler for skiing, our family, together again, was on its way to the Aloha State!

CHAPTER TWENTY

ALOHA

As we all left the plane at Honolulu, Hedy, a friend who was vacationing there, met us with the traditional leis so that we were flower-bedecked like most of the other incoming visitors. A warm breeze embraced us as we walked to the taxi stand – so warm, so soothing and gentle. I supposed the tropic zephyrs would make the heat more bearable for at times.

As our main destination was the Island of Maui, we had time only to drive around Honolulu and drop Hedy off – we planned a longer visit before we finally took the return flight to Vancouver.

There are six islands in the Hawaiian chain – Westerly, Maui, Oahu, Hauai, and Nihau. We wouldn't have time to visit them all this time (I wondered if Alvin had meant we had to see the all). Each has its own character, and one of them is quite remote – no telephone, no cars, no TV!

As we drove Hedy home and did some sightseeing at the same time, Kurt Jr. pointed out the Dole Pineapple company plant; the thought of that juicy fruit made us quite thirsty and Kurt Sr. suggested we stop for a drink.

The tall glass held an exotic Polynesian drink which Hedy warned us was very potent. One was certainly enough! We finished our drinks, dropped Hedy off and headed back to the airport terminal to catch the flight to Maui.

At the airport there were a number of people in the waiting room. What a mixture of Chinese, Japanese, Hawaiian and Caucasian! Some of them were very beautiful.

"Look over there at that girl," I whispered to Vivian. "She must be Tahitian with that long, silky black hair, slim body and such dark eyes." Everybody had such beautiful tans; we looked like ghosts beside them, and hot, uncomfortable ghosts at that, still in our winter clothes.

"You need only a muumuu here. That' the first thing I'll do in Maui, buy a muumuu."

•••

MAUI. Another world. If ever I had come close to Paradise, this was it. The sky was a blue no painter could copy, and palm trees swayed in greeting as we drove to our hotel. Everywhere we saw people wandering along as if there was no other purpose in life but to enjoy oneself.

Vivian and Kurt Jr. were booked at the Sheraton Hotel and Kurt and I had a condo; this way we all had privacy, could visit back and forth and enjoy both beaches. I preferred the beach at the hotel, as the waves were not as high. I still remembered the trouble I'd had in Mexico with the waves – and still hadn't learned to walk out into the surf and then swim back, instead of trying to do it the other way around!

As we watched a group surfing, Kurt said, "How do you like those waves?" It was interesting to watch but I had no desire to join the surfers – not like Kurt Jr., who was fascinated, I noted with some alarm.

"No, please don't," I said as if guessing his thoughts.

"Why not?" he replied. "It's no more dangerous than skiing."

I was glad they had their own place; if he did try it I wouldn't have to watch.

We unpacked and decided to have a swim before dark. The beaches were not crowded as most people were getting ready for dinner, and the water was just perfect. Kurt felt fine, but I watched him constantly as he disappeared behind the waves.

Suddenly, it was dark. There was no twilight in this latitude – day and night happen very quickly. We suddenly realized we'd had nothing to eat all day, and hurried back to get ready for dinner, enjoying the evening air scented with tropical flowers and exotic perfumes.

We joined Kurt Jr. and Vivian at a window seat and watched the exciting scene pass by, enjoying the togetherness we had missed over the recent years.

The menu was quite similar to that of any good restaurant on the mainland, but there was a greater variety of fruit available. But the drinks!

Kurt ignored his diet restrictions and ordered one tall glass after another.

"What was it Irmtrud said we were to order when we were in Hawaii?" he whispered after the waiter had taken our latest order and left.

"I think it's either a Sunset or a Sundowner or something like that.

That first day had passed so quickly, and I fell asleep listening to the waves below my window.

Next morning we were up early, and I made breakfast in our little kitchenette before we walked down to meet Vivian and Kurt Jr. The fifteen-minute walk would do us good, and it was not so hot in the early morning. We passed a number of joggers along the beach, who greeted us in a friendly manner. Everyone seemed so friendly here; I supposed there was no stress in this part of the world, but just the same wondered if there was a hospital nearby.

Vivian and Kurt were not up yet, so we went for a swim. The sky was as blue as it had been the day before, and the water was as warm.

"I don't know if I would like to live here," I said to Kurt as we lay on our bamboo mats later. "I think I prefer the seasons; but it's nice if you have sunshine fourteen days in a row. Do you think it rains here?"

"Sure, they had rain just before we arrived; and it's winter here now, too."

We lazed about like everyone else, waiting for Kurt and Vivian. After a while I was tired of this, and deciding the children had wanted to sleep in, suggested to Kurt that we do some shopping. He closed his eyes just as I made the suggestions, but I knew he'd heard me.

"Shall I go alone?"

"No. I'd better come with you or you'll buy the whole of Maui."

"Well, we need some groceries and also I want to buy some papayas – I really like them." I'd seen them back home in the supermarkets but had not known what they were and had not ventured to try one before.

The shopping center was just around the corner, and I forgot all about papayas when I saw all the colourful muumuus. The dark-haired sales girl was very patient as I had fun trying on one after another, not really knowing what I wanted. I was rummaging through a corner rack and saw, with a shock, Alvin's muumuu! No, not quite the same. I wondered if she had been her before me, if this was the shop where she had bought her Hawaiian dress. Finally, to Kurt's relief, I picked out a blue one and paid for it.

"Let's go have an ice cream somewhere and then phone the kids to see if they want to have lunch with us."

Vivian said, when we called, that they had just had breakfast and wouldn't want lunch, so Kurt and I looked for a snack bar and had a fruit salad. The place was prettily decorated with pictures from the time the whalers were here – lots of bamboo furniture and pretty, dark-haired waitresses. They all looked very Polynesian, wearing a wraparound skirt and halter-top, and a flower behind the ear. I wondered if Eve had looked like that...

"Or was she blonde?" I mused aloud.

"Who?" asked Kurt.

"Eve. You know, I don't know if she was blonde or dark."

Kurt's attention was clearly not on my conversation but rather, on the waitresses as they swayed between the tables, serving customers. I was happy that he felt so well.

The following morning, Vivian phoned; she had spent the whole previous afternoon in the sun and, being a redhead, had been badly burned. We rushed down to the hotel and when we saw how much pain she was in, rented a car and drove to the village of Lanai to see a doctor.

I was convinced now that Eva must have been dark – she was certainly no redhead! Poor Viv was the colour of boiled lobster and swollen over her entire body.

As we drove, I noticed for the first time that people do work in Hawaii, for there was road construction going on that necessitated a detour.

The doctor just smiled when he saw Viv; I supposed he saw a couple of cases like hers in his practice. After giving Viv some injections, creams and pills she felt better almost immediately, but didn't like his advice – stay out of the sun for a few days!

Kurt had an idea for a diversion – "Why don't we find out how we can get to the mountain?" Viv's sunburn, it seemed, was the perfect excuse for his hunger for the *Heilige Berge* to be indulged!

"What mountain?" I asked.

Haleakala, the highest peak on the chain, was within driving distance and we arranged to go there the next day. So the remainder of the afternoon was spent in leisurely walking and shopping for souvenirs.

That evening we took Vivian to a luau, a Hawaiian feast, we'd seen them heating the stones to roast the pig earlier that day. Most people sat on the ground, but we had a table at which we sat and listened to the singers, and watched the girls dancing the hula.

Everybody was in a festive mood and Kurt suddenly took my hand, like all those other lovers (mostly honeymooners) we saw around us. I was glad he felt so obviously well – how could anyone feel otherwise in a setting like this?

We left early next morning to drive up Haleakaia (House of the Sun). It is a very scenic drive along what we were told was the highest access road to the peak anywhere. I was glad Kurt Jr. was driving, and for once Kurt Sr. did not mind.

We stopped at a lookout point to admire the view and I realized how happy Kurt was that finally we could see mountains again! It was a chilly at this altitude and I was glad I had brought sweaters for us all.

At the summit of House of the Sun we read the plaque stating that we were at an altitude of ten thousand and twenty-five feet. "This is the largest of all extinct craters, a twenty miles around and two thousand seven hundred and twenty feet deep." Vivian threw a scrap of paper into the abyss and we watched the wind carry it away into space. Kurt Jr. picked up one of the reddish stones that line the rim to take home for a souvenir. We noted a few other tourists there, enjoying the view – one lady even wore a fur coat against the chilly winds.

Kurt became very quiet, and I suddenly realized that this altitude must be difficult for his heart, so rushed everyone back to the car. He could well have been merely pensive at the sight of the mountains, but I was taking no chances. It was time to turn back, anyway, I reasoned. We had seen everything except the Observatory, which was closed.

The road was a little different from the Squamish highway, and I asked Kurt Jr. how he liked driving. "It's okay," was all he said and I realized I was the one who was nervous, not he. Eleanor Roosevelt had once said, "Don't tell your children that you are afraid if you see them sitting high in an apple tree. If they are not afraid, you have no business telling them that you worry."

When we arrived at the base, we were ready for a drink and some food. While we were eating our pork roast I asked Kurt Jr., "How did it feel driving up the highest road in the world?"

"It's not the highest!"

"That's what is said up there. I don't think there is another road where you can drive your car up to ten thousand feet."

Back at the hotel we decided to go for a swim; it was so warm here, and those warm breezes were most welcome after the cold winds atop Haleakala.

•••

We had decided to celebrate our last day on Maui at the beautiful Sheraton hotel everyone was talking about. It was within easy walking distance, and we set off at sunset, meeting a lot of elegant, beautiful people along the way, each muumuu more beautiful than the last. The men looked fine in white slacks and tropical shirts – Kurt's white and black one set off his tan. In fact, Vivian and I were jealous of both Kurts, who both sported beautiful tans. No one would suspect that Kurt had heart trouble or had recently been hospitalized. We were all thankful that nothing had marred our holiday; at times I had worried, but Kurt was a picture of health and I guessed it had been a good idea to come.

We reached the Sheraton and walked in.

We all stopped talking and just stared. The entrance hall was huge, with high palm trees and exotic plants reaching up to the sky. I wondered if they had built the hotel around the plants or brought them in afterwards.

The waiter, a man with an English accent, showed us to a table beside a pond where flamingos strolled and swans circled as if dancing for us. None of us heard him ask if he could bring us a drink – entranced, we drank up the scene around us until Kurt finally angrily called the waiter over and demanded a drink. "But sir, I was here several times," the waiter protested. We all laughed. "It happens all the time," the waiter said.

We decided to try the Sundowner that we had promised Irmtrud we'd have for her. "If Maui is paradise then this is its headquarters," I said. "Isn't it something?"

"*Ja*, and the prices, too," Kurt replied. "Well, I suppose somebody has to pay for all this!"

A friend of Vivian's arrived while we were having our meal, and as music began playing in the background, asked us if we had any requests for the pianist, who was a friend of hers. I walked over and asked him to play some Viennese waltzes, not really believing he knew any – but to my surprise he gave us the *Blue Danube* and a few others, saying it was a relief to play something different from *Tiny Bubbles*, which everyone requests all the time.

We had a most beautiful evening and I decided that, like Alvin, we'd have to make at least one return visit.

But we were not leaving the islands yet. We still had one whole week in Honolulu, the capital city of Hawaii, known worldwide for the beaches of Waikiki. The beaches were more crowded than those at Maui, and people were lying like sardines in the sun, we saw from our hotel window. Kurt and Vivian had a room on the next floor, and their suite did not overlook the beach. I felt sorry for them until that evening, when I heard drums beating below our window. Then I realized they did not have a better view, but more quiet. I almost wanted to trade with them, but it was for only a few days, after all.

The water was just as warm as in Maui and the waves were maybe a fraction higher, but the beach was so long we could always look for a better spot.

We were all ready to go sightseeing – the statue of Kamehameha and some buildings and maybe the zoo or aquarium were on our list. We had not had a family fight since we arrived on the islands, but now we were divided, with everyone having a different opinion on what to see first. We could have split up, but that would have defeated the purpose of the trip and so we decided that we'd do Honolulu one day, Pearl Harbour the next and Diamond Head the following day. "And if Kurt wants to go skiing," I heard someone say, "there is skiing on the slopes of Mauna Koa in winter." He just laughed.

Honolulu must be one of the busiest cities on earth, so many people coming and going day and night. As we walked we heard – music – suddenly, familiar music, and Kurt followed it just like he had followed it in the Mexican jungle. Somehow they always know he is coming, I thought. We suddenly found ourselves in front of a Bavarian restaurant, and just marched right down the stairs as if someone had commanded us.

Perhaps we were all tired and glad of a chance to sit down, but it seemed as though there was a sense of habit or tradition here, and so we all enjoyed our wiener schnitzel in Honolulu.

In the evening we had a rendezvous with our friend Hedy and her brother and over supper decided to drive to Diamond Head the next day, instead of Pearl Harbour as originally planned. Since her brother lived in Honolulu, he would be our guide; actually, he looked Hawaiian and I wondered if one's features changed if one lived in a place for a long time.

The drive to Diamond Head took us past beaches with waves high as buildings, and we stopped and watched for a while. I could not understand how anyone could ride those waves, but they were doing it and if I had not seen it, I would not have believed it possible.

We had lunch in a beautiful building shaped like a Chinese temple; flowers were everywhere, and there were little ponds spanned by bridges in the garden.

After our tour, Hedy asked us what we had enjoyed most, and we really could not tell her. All we could say was that we would not have wanted to miss any of it.

We were all sure that we would be back again, so decided to leave Pearl Harbour for our next trip to Hawaii and spend the rest of the time at the beach.

Tired, sunburned and happy we arrived in Vancouver. As the plane touched down we looked out the windows and could not believe all the snow that awaited us. It was winter all right – but it seldom snows in this city; rain is more usual, summer or winter.

The taxi could hardly make it up the hill to our house, but when we finally went in we realized suddenly that we were returning only to move house. Everything, or almost everything, was packed and boxes were everywhere. The finality of it hit us all. Suddenly Vivian and Kurt Jr. cried, "Thank you, Dad, for the most beautiful trip," and hugged and kissed their father. I noticed tears running down Viv's cheeks. We all seemed to sense that with Kurt and me moving out of the city it would not be the same anymore.

"Let's make a fire," I said briskly. "After all, it's Christmas in a few days!"

The snow was still falling as I built a fire in the Glass Room fireplace, where the Christmas tree sat ready. It was a small one, in a pot, which I had bought before we left and decided to leave here for our return. But the festive look of the room did not change our moods. Somehow, each one of us sensed we would be drifting apart, that our family era was ending.

•••

Our last Christmas in the old house. We were not left much time to think or get lost in memories as the new owners were moving in New Year's Eve, which was just as well. There were not too many presents; the children had bought Kurt and me each a ski pass for Mount Baker, since we didn't have our cabin on Whistler anymore.

"It was all done before Dad had to go to the hospital," Viv was saying, "but I think an extension can be arranged with the travel office."

"I will be one hundred percent again, you'll see," Kurt was now saying. "I've decided to have an operation."

"An operation!" we all echoed. "What kind of operation?"

"Open heart surgery."

I was glad I was sitting or I would have fallen. "He is in no condition to have surgery," I thought. I knew those operations could be very successful, and I wished he had had it done after his first or second heart attack but now... Well, we all knew that when Kurt said he would do something, he would do it. Although he looked well, Kurt had lost too much weight and sometimes I noticed his breathing was a bit laboured. Perhaps the doctors would talk him out of it.

Oh, God help us all.

•••

The snow held off while we finished the move to our new house. Moving in the middle of winter is insane, especially around Christmas and New Year's. While our friends were all skiing on Whistler, we were moving, but contented ourselves by imagining their reactions to seeing our new house.

We had invited them all for drinks New Year's Day, and I could hardly wait to see the expressions on their faces.

We were so much closer to Whistler now and had such a fantastic view of the mountains. I didn't think any of our friends had been to the

Garibaldi Highlands, since they must have passed it on their way to Whistler, but had never stopped – being in too much of a hurry to reach the slopes.

I was really glad we had bought the house and could see how happy Kurt was. He could hardly wait to get moved and settled in; he was going home to the mountains.

The new furniture looked lovely in the living room, but Kurt did not look at the furniture; his eyes were fixed on the mountains. I felt as I had when we first arrived in Badgastein, surrounded by mountains, quite content. Our search for a retirement retreat had ended; we could not have found a nicer spot.

"Did you know it was actually an Italian, Guiseppi Garibaldi, who came here first, almost a hundred years ago?" Kurt didn't hear my question. He was too busy planning his *Bauernstube*. He called me down to the basement, which was huge, and showed me where he would build this and that and I thought, "Right now he is in no condition to build anything!" As if guessing my thoughts, he said, "After my operation I will be as good as new. I will buy a boat and go fishing and maybe build a house for spec and of course, skiing in the winter. It's only half an hour to Whistler from here."

We did not miss our West Vancouver house at all, and it was fun decorating our beautiful new home.

We were almost finished New Year's Eve, and we walked from one room to another with great satisfaction. We had not always been in agreement in the past, but this time we really harmonized and it showed. It was like starting a marriage – any doubt or disharmonies were gone now.

We both knew and felt that the togetherness was much stronger now, in our golden years. We sat in our den, the fire crackling in the beautiful fireplace and listened to the radio and the people celebrating all over the world. There was the clock pounding out the last chime of midnight as Kurt opened a bottle of champagne. Just the two of us, not needing anyone else as we welcomed 1981 together.

CHAPTER TWENTY-TWO
GOLDEN DAYS

I felt like I was on my honeymoon. Kurt and I had much more time for one another now; there was no stress, and life here was not so hectic. We loved the place more and more every minute.

New Year's Day, our friends came, and each was more surprised than the last but all agreed it was a beautiful spot. One of our friends said right away, "I am going to buy a house here, too!" None of them had known this area existed and I could see that we were envied.

"Why didn't you tell us about this?"

"You sure kept it secret!"

And everyone started talking about their plans. Most wanted to move out of the city.

"Don't you miss Whistler?" Leo asked.

"Why should we? We are so close; you can always stop here after skiing if you feel like it." Kurt served punch and put on some music; it was almost like old times again.

•••

One day Kurt went to Vancouver and came back with a boat. I could not believe it and asked, "Did you have help?"

"Oh, no, it's nothing," he answered as he tried to lift the boat from that trailer. I ran to help, but he showed an incredible strength. I hoped he was not overdoing it.

He kept looking around the house to see what he could do next, and I had to slow him down occasionally and asked him to join me on a walk on the boulevard. We really liked that boulevard. It was so peaceful, and the mountains seemed to follow us wherever we went.

"It's just like being in Austria, don't you think?" Kurt said on one of our walks.

It had started to snow gently when Kurt suddenly said, "I will have my operation in February." He reminded me again; I had almost forgotten about it.

"Before or after your birthday?" Kurt's birthday was February 8.

"After, on February 27."

"What's the rush?" I asked.

"I want it done as soon as possible so I can go skiing again and do everything else."

I did not say anything. I kept telling myself there was nothing to worry about, that those are very successful operations.

As we arrived home, the phone was ringing, and it was Ushi and Erhardt saying they would be coming down to visit us and our new house. They planned to make it for Kurt's birthday, for we had always remembered each other's special days with gifts.

"We like it!" They both said as they arrived.

"It's nicer than your old house," Erhardt said.

"What do you say to the garden?" Kurt asked. "Maybe we could put in a pool if we have money?"

"You sure have the room for it," I remarked. "I can't understand people wanting to move into an apartment."

"Well, wait till you get older and you don't want to cut all that grass."

"I'll never move into an apartment," Kurt answered.

"Erhardt wants to retire to Stuart Lake," Ushi said, "but not me."

Ushi and Erhardt had bought along an article about a reporter who had had heart surgery and handed it to Kurt to read. "Those things are very common now," Erhardt said as he sipped his wine.

"You had better have Agnes read this," Kurt joked. "She is more scared than I."

"Where are your children, now?" they asked us

"Vivian met a producer and he hired her, so she has gone to Hawaii. Kurt Jr. is back in Alberta again."

"So it is just the two of you. What happened to your fighting?"

"We gave that up," Kurt said. "No need for it anymore."

"Come on, sometimes it was fun listening to you two; although sometimes I didn't like it, when you went too far," Ushi replied.

"No more of that you see. We get along wonderfully now. Agnes does not even argue when I say, 'Let's go to Whistler!' In fact, that's where we are going tomorrow."

"Tomorrow!" I asked in astonishment.

"No arguing!" Kurt said immediately; he won that one, all right!

Ushi and Erhardt did not mind the drive out to Whistler since they had not been there since they were stranded there that cold New Year's Eve. Did they get a surprise! We passed by the old house, and all of us looked automatically left when we approached the area. It felt a little strange, not turning down the familiar road. The curtains, our old curtains, were drawn and no water was running into the trough; there were no flowers in the window boxes. Kurt stepped on the gas, as if to drive by fast.

We arrived in the new village and Erhardt immediately began shooting away with the camera that was always hanging from his shoulders. I noticed the sun glinting off his hair, which had gone pure white, a colour most women would love their hairdressers to achieve. Ushi still looked tanned from last year – she never loses her colour. I love these two; they are like our brother and sister. "We do have some nice friends," I thought.

When we tired from walking, we stopped for lunch at Stoney's, one of the new restaurants. We looked in vain for familiar faces.

"It sure has changed," Ushi and Erhardt kept saying.

"*Ja*, but I think it will be nice when it's all finished," Kurt said. "And I am looking forward to skiing Blackcomb."

We sat at the window and had a good view of the village square, all paved in stone and bordered by stores on all sides, side-by-side just like villages back home, when I was a little girl. There was even a clock on one of the towers of a building.

After lunch we drove around a bit, noticing all the building still going on and the people working feverishly; but we found no one at home when we knocked at familiar doors on Whistler, so we decided to drive back to Garibaldi.

Every time we opened the front door of our new house, we felt waves of contentment and happiness wash over us, and we paused as usual to have a look at the mountains before going in. Yes, they were still there.

Ushi and Erhardt stayed a few more days and we went for walks together, talked a lot about old times and the future – which meant we could spend more time on Stuart Lake. Kurt planned to take the new boat up there this summer and I could hardly wait to get there.

We drove them to the airport and it was a lovely drive, as Kurt amazed us all as he stopped without being asked at spots where Erhardt could take lovely pictures. He is in no big rush now, and was willing to take time to see the view and beauty himself, for once. We sat beside the big stone on which everyone who passed had written their name. Too bad we had nothing to write with, as it would have been fun to add our names.

And so we said goodbye once again to our dear friends as the airplane flew them to their home in Prince George. After seeing them off, we chose to spend a little time in Vancouver, and I was amazed again as Kurt steered his car toward Robsonstrasse and decided to go window-shopping with me.

"If this continues," I thought, "it will be something I did not expect!" We strolled hand in hand along the street, stopping here and there. Just then, Kurt caught sight of a beautiful Cameo for my necklace and asked me if I would like it. I thought it was beautiful, so we went in and he bought it!

"What's the occasion?" I asked. "It's not my birthday."

"I know. Just enjoy it and don't ask too many questions."

Afterwards we went to the Mozart Café to have some pastry and coffee and suddenly I was back in Austria at the time Kurt and I had met and he told me the story of his capture. I had just asked him to finish telling me everything, for he never really had completed that long-ago story, when the waitress came over and asked, in German, if we would like more Kuchen. It gave me a shock to have her fit so neatly into our long-ago picture!

We sat there, talking, for quite a while, watching the world go by. Kurt was in no hurry to leave. If this is retirement, it's wonderful! We watched old couples and young couples sitting and sipping their coffee, some smiling happily and other looking as if they had just had an argument. I would have loved to tell those later, "Don't do it. It really isn't worth it." I was just so happy I would have liked to tell the whole world about it.

When we finally did leave to make the long drive to Garibaldi, the waitress looked quite astonished at the large tip received!

•••

Vivian and Kurt came home for their father's birthday. They enjoyed the house and their new rooms, and we enjoyed them. Kurt Jr. told us he was planning to move back to Vancouver; Alberta was not so good anymore, and Grande Prairie was more of a ghost town than a boomtown. Projects which should have gone ahead did not materialize and everyone was moving out. He had landed a job, as an estimator with a Vancouver firm and will live in Vivian's house. There was enough room there, even if Viv was coming back after her Hawaiian engagement. I was happy to hear that one of the children would be closer to home, and it appeared father approved as well.

Vivian had bought dad a captain's hat and few other things for his new boat; Kurt Jr. gave him a few books on how to navigate his new vessel. Friends came by to wish Kurt well on his 61st in this life; Kurt enjoyed it all.

The children decided to stay on for Kurt's operation, so that they could visit him in the hospital, and no doubt it pleased father even though he protested that it wasn't necessary.

CHAPTER TWENTY-THREE

The day of Kurt's operation was a bright, sunny February day and as I watched the clock that morning I thought of the previous day's activities.

We had driven with Kurt to the hospital; I had decided to stay at Viv's place so I wouldn't have to make the long drive from Garibaldi to Vancouver each day. We all had lunch together, Kurt and I and the children, at a nearby restaurant and afterwards went to St. Paul's Hospital, Vivian carrying her father's suitcase and Kurt Jr., his robe. When Kurt settled in and the nurse allowed us to his room, I was disappointed to see that his view consisted of a stone wall. But Kurt didn't seem to mind and the other patient, who had recently had his own operation, was equally cheerful.

We saw him comfortably settled in by the nurses, then, assured he didn't want for anything, left for home.

•••

It was eight o'clock when I got up the following day: Kurt must be in the operating room now. I wished that they had let me stay at the hospital but the doctor suggested it would be better to be at home, near the telephone, and they would call as soon as the operation was over.

The clock seemed to move so slowly today. Vivian was cleaning the house and Kurt Jr. had already left for work at his new job, but said he would be home for lunch.

Lunchtime came and still there was no call from the hospital. I was restless. "Why don't they phone? It's been hours. Surely the operation must be over! I will phone them."

So I did.

"They are still operating," the nurse said.

Still operating! Five hours!

Kurt Jr. was just getting ready to leave for work again when the phone rang. Viv and I both leapt for it; I was there first.

"We are sorry...."

The receiver fell to the floor.

From what seemed a long way away, I heard Vivian screaming over and over, "No, Daddy, NO! Oh no, Daddy, No!"

Her screaming brought Kurt Jr. running back down the stairs; trying to be brave, he held us both in his arms.

Afterward, people kept coming – friends and neighbours we had known over the years came, trying to say something, trying to do something to ease the loss.

Late at night, we crawled into our beds, each wanting to help the other in their grief, and unable even to help ourselves.

Unable to sleep, I stood at he window. I had never realized what a lovely view Vivian had from her house. I realized I had never before spent the night at her house. I just stood there, gazing at the sea of lights below me, wondering where Kurt's spirit may be now.

Suddenly there was no feeling of time passing; everything was unreal, dreamlike. The sun didn't seem to be shining for me; though others would comment on its warmth, I didn't feel it.

There was the funeral to go through.

Kurt had wished aloud so often to have his ashes scattered at Whistler, but it took a long time before I was ready to carry out that final request.

Easter Sunday, we returned his soul to the mountain that had held it all along – and my heart rested there with him, on the constant *Heilige Berge.*